D1827236

Performance
Measurement for Charities

ULB
QT

Performance Measurement for Charities

David Wise

ICSA Publishing
The Official Publishing Company of
The Institute of Chartered Secretaries and Administrators

First published 1995 by
ICSA Publishing Limited
Campus 400, Maylands Avenue
Hemel Hempstead
Hertfordshire HP2 7EZ

Typeset in 10/12½pt Palatino
by Dorwyn Ltd, Rowlands Castle, Hants

Printed and bound in Great Britain by
Biddles Ltd, Guildford and King's Lynn

British Library Cataloguing in Publication Data

A catalogue record for this book is available from
the British Library
ISBN 1-872860-78-8

1 2 3 4 5   99 98 97 96 95

Contents

Series editor's foreword

In the United States a considerable body of academic literature has been presented which identifies the voluntary sector as a distinct area of study. There has also been an outpouring of books on 'best practice' and 'how to do it'.

In the United Kingdom we currently do not enjoy this depth of academic research; instead we have a few pockets of academic researchers. In addition there are a limited number of texts outlining best practice, ranging from small factual briefing notes that are soon outdated to large professional 'information texts'.

I believe the United Kingdom needs a series of quality books that will move beyond the 'handbook' while providing practical advice – a series that could offer a strong grounding of theoretical debate and pragmatic analysis.

This series attempts to fulfil that need. Written by a multi-disciplinary team of academics and practitioners, the series aims to breach the gap between theoretical texts and practical guides. We have sought to explore and identify the specific characteristics of the voluntary sector, thus enabling those working either in or with that sector to fulfil their tasks more effectively.

After the launch of the first books in the series I expressed the hope that many more would follow. One quickly did on fund-raising by the 'doyen' of the field Redmond Mullin. Two more have now been launched – Charities and Taxation written by the Founder Chair of the Charities Finance Directors Group, Adrian Randall, with my colleague at South Bank University Stephen Williams and Performance Measurement for Charities – authored by David Wise, the Course Director of the MSc Charity Finance at South Bank University.

More books are planned to cover topics from Human Resource Management, internal control to quality management and corporate governance.

Preface

I spent my early career in the private and public sectors and did not become involved with charities in any depth until the end of the 1980s when I carried out a series of value-for-money studies for the then Department of Health and Social Security.

At the time I had expected to find a high sense of dedication and assumed that this would give all concerned a common goal and ideal. I was unprepared, therefore, for the degree of internal politics which seems to exist in many charities. Charities by definition have defined charitable objects which generally seek to further the interests of the beneficiaries of the charity. But it seemed that there were often hidden agendas and that in some respects charities seemed no less unworldly than commercial businesses and perhaps rather less clearly focused.

At the same time, I was surprised to find that many charities, though outside the public sector, had cultures similar to those in government bodies; terms and conditions of employment were often based on Civil Service scales; financial control systems were similar to public service systems, often good in control of economy but poor in terms of output planning and performance measurement; the relationship between a charity's trustees and its full-time managers was similar in some ways to that between the council members and the staff members in local government, with often a proliferation of committees and sub-committees.

I was unprepared, too, for the sheer size and enormous variation which exists in the charity sector, which makes generalisation so dangerous. The not-for-profit organisation seems to me to be much more difficult to manage than a commercial company and the best charities have much to teach the typical business in terms of personnel management, motivation and quality management; they have been tackling the difficulty of measuring performance in qualitative and non-financial terms for years, while many commercial businesses have only recently become interested in such non-financial measures.

Since my initial work with charities I have spent increasing time in the field and took on the position of course director of the South Bank Business School's MSc course in Charity Finance in 1992. This has enabled me to take this opportunity to explore the problems of measuring performance in charities; the reasons why performance measurement in charities is different from, and perhaps more important than, that in businesses; and what measures are used. It is associated with the wider question of accountability in charities, which is also touched on here. The aim of the exercise is to help the trustees and managers of charities to monitor their performance, to seek to recognise good and bad practices, and to suggest ways in which the accountability and performance of the sector might be improved.

Timing is propitious for two reasons. The years 1992 and 1993 saw new legislation introduced to regulate charities in England and Wales; early in 1995 a new Statement of Recommended Accounting Practice was issued (Accounting Standards Board 1995). The increased interest in the sector coincided with the publication by the Home Office in 1993 of research by Barry Knight entitled *Voluntary Action*, which claimed to be the most ambitious study of voluntary action and voluntary organisations since Beveridge completed his work on the welfare state with his book *Voluntary Action* in 1948 (Knight 1993, p. x) and in 1993 Hemmington Scott published its first annual guide to UK charities (*The Henderson Top 1000 Charities 1993*), which gives comparative data on income, funds and expenditure and claims to be the prime information source on UK charities, thus providing a greater bank of readily available financial statistics than was previously accessible.

In 1994 the first titles in the ICSA Charities Management series (of which this book is part) appeared, with the aim of providing both practical advice and also a strong grounding of theoretical debate and pragmatic analysis of the voluntary sector. I am grateful to all the authors of the series for their advice and for the good example which they have set. I should also like to thank the students on the South Bank course from whom I have learned so much.

Introduction

Performance – accomplishment, achievement, act, carrying out, completion, conduct, consummation, discharge, execution, exploit, feat, fulfilment, work. Measurement – appraisal, assessment, calculation, calibration, computation, estimation, evaluation, judgement, mensuration, metage, survey, valuation.

(Collins Thesaurus, 1992)

The charity sector

This book is written for those who manage and are responsible for organisations in the voluntary sector in general and charities in particular. I do not intend to try to define this sector precisely, if only because it is practically impossible to do so. It is roughly that sector which is neither the private sector nor the public sector. It consists of those organisations which are neither public organisations using moneys voted by Parliament nor private businesses working with their owners' capital and with funds available through the corporate finance market. This definition cannot be strictly applied because there are increasingly large overlaps between sectors; as Barry Knight (1993) observes:

in 1989 it was becoming apparent that public, private, and voluntary were no longer discrete categories. Public authorities were being pressed to charge for services, market test parts of their operations, and set up charitable trusts to help them make ends meet. Private firms were increasingly doing what public organisations used to do and also play a greater part in what charities used to do. Charities and voluntary organisations were beginning to bid for contracts, sometimes in competition with the private and public organisations. Those in receipt of public money had to begin to assimilate the language of the Financial Management Initiative, and behave more like businesses in generating their income.

1

In general I am writing with charities in mind. Registered charities at least give a clearly defined data base, though legal form is not a clear guide. Most of the larger charities tend to be formed as companies limited by guarantee so that their accountability is regulated by the Companies Acts, while many of the largest charities, such as the British Council or the Arts Council, may be thought of as part of the public sector.

Nor is there any clear limitation on activities which may qualify for charitable status. The government has declined to define charity by statutory means – preferring to rely on the courts to apply their judgement to principles set out as long ago as 1891 by Lord Macnaghten (which themselves related to a preamble to the Charitable Uses Act of 1601) – on the grounds that this 'might put at risk the flexibility of the present law which is both its greatest strength and its most valuable feature' (Home Office 1989).

The charity sector for the purpose of this book could be more narrowly limited to what the UK Central Statistical Office (CSO 1993) calls 'general charities' which are regarded as part of the personal sector for national accounts purposes and which exclude some specialist bodies (universities, friendly societies and trades unions), bodies much of whose consumption is offset by sales such as tuition fees or rent (other colleges and schools in the private sector and housing associations), and bodies where information is not readily available (ex-corporation duty bodies such as motoring organisations and city livery companies, clubs and societies, and places of worship).

Overall the CSO estimated that 171,242 UK charities fell into this category, 143,434 of these being in England and Wales. The size distribution of charities is highly skewed; CSO estimates based on Charity Commission returns show that those organisations with an income of up to £100,000 account for 89% of charities but only 7.3% of charities' income, while those with an income of over £10 million account for 0.2% of charities but 36.9% of overall income.

Performance

Commercial businesses have always been interested in efficiency in the narrow sense of profitability because the rewards of the owners and the continuity of the business are dependent on profit. The government's Financial Management Initiative, started in the 1980s, has led to increasing concern with value-for-money measurement in the public sector; this in turn has led to a number of efficiency scrutinies and the development of a raft of performance indicators in public services such as the National Health Service and education.

There seems to have been less attention paid to performance measurement in those mainstream charities which may be described as voluntary organisations. There is less certainty about what value for money means in not-for-profit organisations and how it might be measured.

There is concern, however, that increasing demand for better accountability will increase costs and reduce efficiency in charities. The smaller charity in particular cannot take advantage of economies of scale which are open to the larger charity and may expect to have to devote a relatively larger share of its resources to matters of security and stewardship.

This book aims to explore some of these questions more fully and in particular to

- consider differences between charities and other private or public sector organisations which affect accountability and performance measurement;
- consider empirical evidence of the extent to which performance measures are used in charities;
- suggest approaches to value-for-money measurement and related performance indicators in charities, and thus to identify trends and benchmarks for comparison and control purposes;
- consider differences in performance within the sector; and
- suggest how managers should improve accountability and the performance of their own charities and of the charitable sector generally.

There has been a tendency for performance measurement to be seen as the province of the expert, the economist or the accountant. The need in thousands of charities both large and small is to implement simple and useful measurement procedures which will enable managers to make badly needed improvements in value for money. This book aims to give an overview of the basics and concepts of performance measurement and a practical and straightforward guide to the design and use of performance measurement. The importance of the subject is introduced in Chapter 1, while Chapter 2 explains differences between charities and businesses and how this affects aspects of accountability and performance measurement. Chapter 3 sets out a framework for considering performance and the concepts of value-for-money assessment.

The important first principle of developing objectives from a vision of the charitable objects of an organisation and using these to establish objectives for unit managers is discussed in Chapter 4, while Chapter 5 looks at the basic ingredients of performance measures by which to measure economy, efficiency and effectiveness. Chapter 6 describes how to use budget procedures to motivate managers and to reinforce their planning and control of performance.

The structure of the charity sector is referred to in Chapter 7, which looks at aspects of cooperation between charities and opportunities for benchmarking so that best practices can be more widely applied by charities, while Chapter 8 recaps on the ground covered and emphasises the need to distinguish operational performance measures within a charity from the longer-term strategic performance of the charity as a whole. Chapter 9 draws some general lessons from management information practices in the sector and summarises the main findings, and Chapter 10 reproduces, with changes in name, some case studies to stimulate thought on how the principles outlined in the book might be applied in practice. The case studies may also encourage readers to reflect on the means which could be used, and indeed have been used, to measure and improve performance. As in most aspects of management, it is not to be expected that there is one right way of doing things. The case studies are meant to suggest how theoretical concepts might be applied to real-life problems and to illustrate the complex and sometimes conflicting requirements that such concepts help to resolve.

1 Why measure performance in charities?

Nobody ever believes that his own performance is measurable. Each of us discerns in ourselves intangible, even undemonstrable, and certainly unquantifiable virtues. What we do, we feel, is so much more than any accountant could ever reduce to a set of figures.

(Parris 1994)

National wealth

Quite apart from the need for managers to measure performance, to which this book is addressed, the performance of the charity sector is itself of general significance to the national economy and to the well-being of us all. The UK Central Statistical Office (CSO), as part of the drive to improve national statistics, is in the process of mounting a wide-ranging survey of charities, which are a main component in the personal sector of the national accounts. The charity sector's importance will be better quantified after the results become available from 1996, but it has been estimated that the sector accounts for some 3% of gross domestic product (GDP) and is increasing because of the changing role which government expects it to play. The GDP estimates in turn affect the UK contribution to the European Union budget. Similarly, UK charities are involved with much international work, which needs to be taken into account in balance-of-payments calculations. For all these reasons, it is unsatisfactory that the performance of the charity sector remains so elusive and ill defined.

The 1990/91 survey of charities commissioned by the CSO estimated the population of general charities in the UK as 97,478, with income in 1991 of £9.1 billion and expenditure of £8.5 billion. Staff costs alone in 1991 were £3.1 billion. The Charity Commissioners' report (1994, for example) show that more charities are registered each year than are removed from the register, so the number of charities is not only large but also seems to be growing. The figures are also likely to be grossly understated in so far as they are based simply on accounting figures of income and expenditure, ignoring the labour used (and benefits received by society) from volunteer workers giving their time and efforts for little or no financial reward.

The activities of volunteer workers, in organisations such as the Red Cross or the Women's Royal Voluntary Service, for example, improve the well-being of our society greatly, but this increase in wealth is not financially quantified and does not reflect properly in national statistics. Voluntary work is significant. The 1987 General Household Survey (Matheson 1990) undertaken for the Voluntary Services Unit of the Home Office showed that 25% of women and 21% of men were doing voluntary work and that about a third of those doing such work did so at least once a week on average.

In 1993 the Charity Commission for England and Wales registered 12,559 charities (compared with 4,681 in 1992). It is true that the 1993 figure was exceptionally high because it included 3,326 Women's Institutes and 2,735 pre-school playgroups and other small charities now required to register, but in all recent years the number of new charities registering has greatly exceeded the number taken off the register, with the result that the number registered in England and Wales, 170,932 in 1993, continues to rise.

Public relations

It follows from the size of the figures alone that it is important that we should know how the charity sector is performing and the extent to which it provides value for money. Moreover, charities play an important part in the delivery of a wide range of public services. A large proportion of the population is directly involved with charities – as members, volunteers or beneficiaries – or indirectly supports charities as taxpayers. The performance of charities matters both economically and socially. But it is difficult to be precise about how well this sector is performing.

John Argenti (1993) writes:

Would crime, disablement, poverty, our inner cities be tackled best by a government NPO [non-profit-making organisation], or one run by the Church, or a secular charity, or a self-help cooperative? We have no idea. Is voluntary contribution the best source of succour for those millions starving in Africa? We do not know. Why not? Because we cannot measure, and therefore cannot compare, the performance of any of the various types of NPO.

He continues:

If we cannot measure the performance of NPOs we cannot know if we need them at all or whether we would be better off without them – perhaps they are indeed just an outmoded form of human organisation left over from Queen Victoria's golden age. We cannot arrange them in a meaningful performance league table as we can with companies. We cannot tell whether they are being managed well or badly – or not at all.

Argenti's personal view is that 'well over half of Britain's top NPOs . . . currently make no worthwhile contribution to our national life'. This demonstrates another reason for charities to measure performance. It allows charities to defend themselves against such claims. Traditionally, charities, like the public sector generally, have been good at accounting for their expenditure and income but have not concerned themselves too much with the results of the expenditure and with, to use the current jargon, outputs and outcomes. Lack of measurement means that the sector does not promote its own interests as well as it should and that those working in charities do not always receive the recognition which they deserve.

Finally, performance measurement methods are not now expected just at the top of an organisation. They are increasingly considered a responsibility of line managers at the unit level allowing even middle managers to demonstrate that they are working effectively and giving good value.

Management of charities

Most important for the purposes of this book, managers and trustees cannot know whether they are providing value for money or whether the charity is improving unless there are some measures of performance in place. Measurement is used to indicate whether there is a need for improvement in the first place as well as to assess whether improvement efforts are making progress. Often, in fact, measurement has a dramatic impact on performance simply because the impact of feedback on those measured is so powerful.

The reasons which have been advanced for measuring performance in the public sector (Hyndman and Anderson 1991) apply equally to the management of charities:

Without information about what is being achieved (outputs) and what it is costing (inputs), it is impossible to make efficiency resource allocations . . . These allocation decisions rely on a range of performance measures which, if unavailable, may lead managers to allocate resources based on subjective judgement, personal whim or in response to political pressure.

Without performance measures managers will not know: the extent to which operations are contributing to effectiveness and efficiency; when diagnostic interventions are necessary; how the performance of their organisation compares with similar units elsewhere; and how their performance has changed over time. Such information is the foundation for good management . . .

Government may require performance information to decide how much to spend in the public sector and where, within the sector, it should be allocated. In particular they will be interested to know what results may be achieved as a consequence of a particular level of funding, or to decide whether or not a service could be delivered more effectively and efficiently in the private sector.

The modern management perception of total quality management is one of continuous improvement. It has gone beyond the idea of providing a service to a static predetermined standard but recognises that, in a competitive and changing world, successful organisations must continually improve the value that they give to their customers. This is perhaps a private sector perception, though it has been borrowed by the public sector under the government's Financial Management Initiative, and for that reason it will be considered again in a later chapter.

Where organisations exist without the objective of making profit, it may be argued that management can take place without the measurement of performance. Often management has to take decisions on the basis of a hunch. It may not be possible to quantify expectations or to compare results with those expectations. The organisational situations which may arise in states of uncertainty can be illustrated by a matrix (based on Open University 1993, Unit 2) as shown in Figure 1.1.

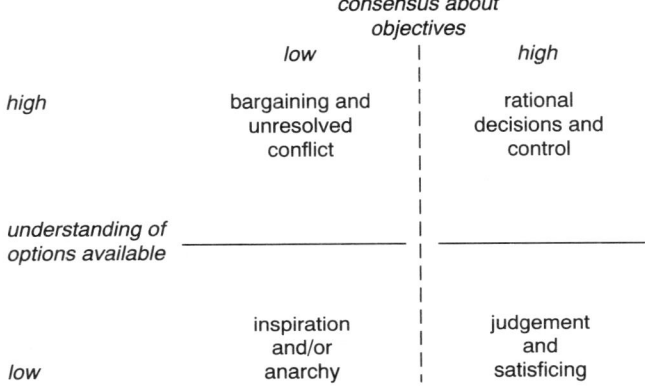

Figure 1.1 Decision-making in circumstances of uncertainty

There are organisations – perhaps religions are an example – where, by the nature of things, there can be no certainty as to outcomes or to the comparative costs and benefits of alternative means. Management must depend largely on ritual and on faith in such circumstances.

In business organisations, where profit optimisation is an important influence towards goal congruence, it may be easier to establish consistent aims and to evaluate alternative strategies. In a charity, which does not have so clear a unifying goal of profitability, managements have to work harder to provide a framework for rational decision-making and control by establishing consensus about objectives and a clear understanding of options available.

This book is written in the belief that practical performance measurement is a tool that should be accessible to all trustees and managers; that it can be applied by almost all managers in any organisation and that the use of such tools can have a profound impact on performance.

Conclusions and key points

This chapter has identified a number of reasons why performance management is important for charities. The voluntary sector is certainly large, even though its exact size is uncertain, and its activities are significant to the national economy. For that reason alone, we should know more about the performance of the sector.

The Central Statistical Office is in the process of collecting more information with which it will be possible to improve national statistics. Even so, it is unlikely that it will be feasible to attempt to quantify that large non-financial element of volunteer labour, which has an opportunity cost and gives a valuable service to charity beneficiaries. Financial statistics and accounts alone will not be sufficient to convey the extent of the advantage to the nation of the voluntary sector.

Performance measures are therefore needed to allow the sector to justify its existence to the public at large and to the government of the day. Unless performance measures are in place, it is difficult for the charity sector to counter criticisms as a whole or for individual charities to refute accusations of poor management and ineffectiveness.

More than that; measurement is essential to the process of management. The management aphorism 'What gets measured gets done' expresses the fact that measurement enables and motivates managers to take effective action. Similarly, the concept of continuous improvement, which is essential to total quality management, cannot be applied without defining and measuring performance. Performance measurement allows management to receive early warning of risk; to make comparisons of performance over time, between units and between charities; to link the efforts of all concerned towards common aims; to demonstrate good performance to stakeholders; and to research new or experimental methods.

Rational management decisions and controls require good knowledge of the objectives of an organisation and also of the comparative effects of alternative actions available to meet the objectives. Because of the number of different interests in some charities it is not always easy to reach consensus about objectives, nor is it easy in many charitable areas to compare the costs and benefits of alternative actions available. Managements which need to demonstrate that they are giving value for money and that they are making good use of the resources at their disposal do therefore have to try hard to establish agreed aims and to measure the inputs and outputs of the processes under their control. Subsequent chapters in this book are designed to deal with these tasks.

2 Why can't a charity be more like a business?

> An individual who intends only his own gain is led by an invisible hand to promote an end which was no part of his intention. Nor is it always the worse for the society that it was no part of it. By pursuing his own interest he frequently promotes that of the society more effectually than when he really intends to promote it. I have never known much good done by those who affected to trade for the public good.
>
> (Adam Smith, *The Wealth of Nations*, 1776, quoted by Friedman 1980)

Philanthropy in the market economy

The operation of the market is fundamental to commercial businesses in two respects. First, the financing of business activity takes place in the context of financial markets competing for funds, so that only those businesses which can promise a return commensurate to the risk involved can expect to receive financial support. Second, businesses must create wealth by providing goods or services of greater value to their customers than the cost of those goods and services – this wealth or profit being returned to reward the investors who took the risk.

The above quotation from Adam Smith sums up the view that, left to itself, the market will best satisfy the joint and several needs of a society. Yet philanthropic views have also recognised that it is repugnant that those unable to afford or to understand basic requirements should be unable to benefit through their inability to compete.

For example, Professor Brian Abel-Smith (1976) described how 'through the centuries, the common law of Europe and America recognised the maintenance of the common health as one of the great tasks of society. . . . The doctor . . . was not free to select or to reject patients at will'. And he quoted from Berg (1945):

As one who follows a common calling the doctor held himself ready to serve all in need to the limit of his capacity. Nor was inability to pay a valid excuse for the refusal of his service. The law recognised him as a kind of unofficial servant of the community and exempted him from the ordinary rules of the market. . . . To insure adequacy of service, a special rule of law was decreed for the physician: he was permitted to charge different fees to patients differently situated . . . It elevated medicine above commerce, broke the pecuniary connection between the doctor's services and his reward, and gave legal recognition to the principle that persons were to be served according to their needs, that charges were to be assessed in terms of ability to pay.

This form of income distribution performed some rough justice, rather along the lines of Robin Hood. But it is clearly rough justice that the rich sick should subsidise the poor sick when the rich healthy would be better placed to do so. Perhaps it also places too much power in the hands of the service provider, in this case the doctor, rather than the person in need, the patient.

Customer power

Almost by definition, in charities as in many professions, the customer is in a weak position relative to the supplier. The undesirable aspects of this, combined with the economic separation of the service provider from the recipient, are well illustrated in an article by the professor of health services management at Nottingham University:

Most [doctors] still use clinical freedom – the need to provide whatever treatment an individual patient requires – as an excuse for ducking their management responsibilities: they treat patients but it is up to others to provide the money. . . . There is never enough money at any one time to meet demand; the job of everyone involved is to try to make whatever is available go as far as possible.

He then expresses concern about how patients are treated, whether they are made welcome and their privacy respected, and so on, and continues:

But the real problem about doctors is that no serious attempt is made to manage their clinical performance, despite the expenditure of countless millions on such procedures as clinical audit. It beggars belief that some hundreds of pounds was spent last year on consultants' merit pay and clinical audit combined, without any shred of accountability attaching to its use. Put crudely, nobody other than the doctor is regarded as having any right to know what the effect of that expenditure has on the way doctors perform. (Caines 1994)

This weakness of the 'customer' in not-for-profit situations is one reason why charities require special treatment and why they should be subject to requirements of accountability in some respects more onerous than those applied to commercial businesses under the Companies Acts.

Accountability

Those concerned with charitable work sometimes question the increasing burdens of accountability placed on trustees and managers by the changes in legislation. It is possible to respond to such questions empirically by pointing to the major charity frauds and financial scandals which appear in the press from time to time and the anecdotal evidence of more widespread minor financial irregularities in very small local voluntary bodies, all of which suggests that cash does not always flow smoothly through a charity from the donors to the beneficiaries.

Shareholders in commercial businesses expect to balance the conflicts of risk and return whenever they invest their money in a business. We may properly expect such shareholders to exercise due caution with regard to their money and they are assisted in their risk-taking by a large infrastructure of corporate and financial analysts, investment advisers and city commentators. The donors who contribute to charities are not looking for a financial return, of course, and they are usually less well equipped than shareholders to take decisions on costs and benefits; while the beneficiaries of charitable activities are hardly ever in a position to judge whether they receive value for money.

Corporate finance cycles

The structure of the market in which commercial businesses operate is one which regulates itself in economic terms through two basic feedback mechanisms (Figure 2.1(a)). On a strategic level, a

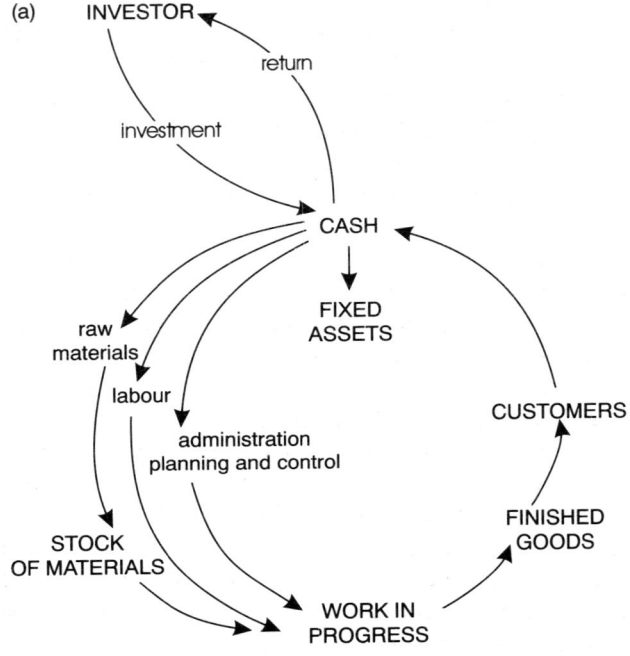

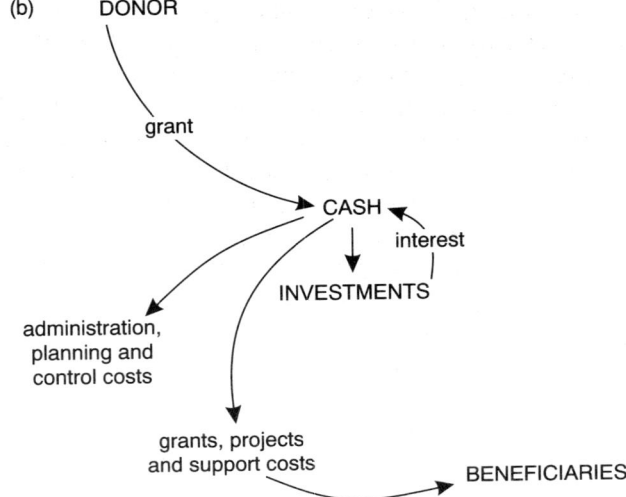

Figure 2.1 Movement of funds in (a) a business; (b) a charity

commercial business relies on external investors to provide finance for the firm. Unless those investors receive a satisfactory return on their investment, the firm will be unlikely to gain access to further finance. On a tactical level, a commercial business must sell products or services to its customers with a value greater than the cost of those goods or services; unless it does so it will not make a profit and will not be able to sustain a return to its investors.

The investment cycle of corporate finance in a commercial business, whereby the investor provides cash which is used to make a profit from which the investor is rewarded by interest, dividend or capital gain, does not operate in a charity (Figure 2.1(b)). Nor does the trading cycle, whereby inputs of labour, materials and overheads are converted into goods or services, which are worth more to a customer than the cost to produce them, apply to the not-for-profit sector (though the spread of contractual arrangements between government and voluntary bodies, whereby the amount of government grant is tied to delivery of services, does seek to provide a feedback loop similar to the price mechanism – but at the same time risks turning such charities into mere agents of the state, as indeed is recommended by Knight 1993).

A commercial business links its corporate financing to the continued operation of its revenue-earning activities by investment in fixed and intangible assets which support and sustain those activities. A charity tends to seek continuity and stability of income by maintaining a reserve of charitable funds as investments to provide a source of support for future service funding levels. Investment appraisal is a key concern in corporate finance; investment management and reserve levels are major strategic concerns for charity managers. The importance of investment management is illustrated by the analysis of the largest charities' balance sheets, based on 2,071 largest charities in the Hemmington Scott 1992 charities data base (see Table 2.1). Compared with private sector companies, charities have much greater investments and higher levels of liquidity. Of course, many charities do not have the benefit of investments and reserves and must rely on regular donors to maintain their activities.

Charities in this situation must pay great attention to how they are viewed by society, government and other potential donors. Where a charity is endowed with funds producing investment

Table 2.1 Combined balance sheets of the largest charities

	1992		1991	
	£m	%	£m	%
Fixed assets	**5,586**	22	5,622	24
Investments	**17,410**	70	15,952	67
Net current assets	**−237**	−1	−442	−2
Liquid assets	**2,136**	9	2,538	11
Total funds	**24,895**	100	23,669	100

income, though the trustees are responsible for the proper use of the funds, the power of the managers is that much greater. The managers of the Wellcome Trust, for example, which is the richest charity in the UK, exercise enormous muscle within the limits imposed by their trust deed. Having such large resources, they could afford to ignore donors and might see little need to be accountable to the public for the use of such resources. The compilers of the Henderson top charities guide have reported that they came across many secretive charitable foundations, which resented being asked to produce accounting information notwithstanding the fact that they were registered charities with the tax benefits attached to charitable status.

In any event, the public does not need to worry about the efficiency of private sector companies, because (except where companies are able to exploit monopoly powers, in which case the public interest may be protected by the Monopolies and Mergers Commission) the competition of the market ensures that inefficient companies will disappear – taken over by a predator or, as a last resort, wound up. The public may rightly question who ensures that the enormous resources held by charities are efficiently used for the public good.

The trading cycle and costing

The illustration above of how funds move round the trading cycle in a commercial business helps to explain the importance, for business organisations, of costing and accounting principles.

The accounting systems in a business must collect all the costs applicable to a period and offset them against the income of the period to ensure that the value of goods and services provided exceeds the cost of supplying them – that is, to ensure that the business is operating profitably.

Where many goods and services are provided, this implies a costing system which can take all the various elements of cost – labour, material, light and heat, printing, stationery and so on – and attribute those costs to the units of sale. In a retail business this may be easy in theory because a high proportion of cost consists of the direct cost of goods sold. Even so, there will be a great variety of different products to control and there will be a need to apportion common costs to individual products in order to judge whether each product is making a proper contribution to the profit of the business.

In service industries, the most suitable units of output may be more difficult to determine. Public transport businesses have the concept of passenger miles. British Airways, for example, measures not just passengers carried and tonnes of cargo carried but also, among other things, available tonne kilometres and revenue tonne kilometres.

The point is that businesses make an effort to calculate their unit costs. Such costs are an aid to controlling profit and pricing policies but they also give a measure of efficiency. One way of securing competitive advantage is to try to achieve lower costs than competitors. Comparative unit costs, over time or between businesses, are an important performance indicator. Charities do not usually need to establish a profitable selling price for their services; consequently it is rare to find well-designed costing systems which show the unit cost of services provided. Yet, without such a concept, it is hardly possible to talk of cost-effectiveness at all.

The trading cycle and accounting principles

The illustration of the corporate finance and trading cycles above emphasises the central position of cash in the business process. The value of a business or an investment is the present value of all the expected future cash flows. Over the complete life of a business or project, the profit is the same as the difference between cash invested and cash realised from the investment, making allowance for the timing of the cash.

Of course, a business executive or investor cannot wait until the final completion of the business to know what profit or loss has been made. Accountants compute, for each accounting period, exactly what profit or loss has arisen. To do so, they must consider not just what cash has been received and paid but also what income and expenditure relates precisely to the period in question because there are important timing differences between cash and profit in any one accounting period. Accountants call this the *matching* or the *accruals* concept.

The concept of current expenditure, applicable wholly to the accounting period in question, and capital expenditure, which will benefit many future accounting periods, is vital to this computation of profit, since capital expenditure is not charged against income when it is spent but is written off slowly by way of instalments based on the estimated life of the expenditure – known as *depreciation*.

In computing profit, accountants also assume that the entity will continue into the foreseeable future – the *going concern* concept. They also take a cautious view in their calculations in that – in keeping with the notion of prudence – they make provision for all known liabilities even if the amounts are not exactly certain and have to be estimated; but they ignore uncertain future income.

Profit, therefore, is simply an accountant's calculation. Different accountants may make different judgements or estimates and produce quite different profit calculations. The recent concerns about so-called creative accounting have highlighted the various means by which businesses may seek, deliberately or otherwise, to manipulate their figures in order to overstate or understate their profits. These creative accounting devices all stem from the need to adjust cash transactions, which are certain, to an accruals basis for profit calculation, which is estimated.

For a business which needs to determine its profit, these accounting adjustments and estimates are essential. Accountants, who are steeped in these concepts, have recently been very successful in introducing these ideas into the not-for-profit sector, where their relevance is by no means so clear.

For example, life-boats acquired by the Royal National Lifeboat Institution (RNLI) are clearly capital expenditure in that they should last for many years, but there seems little point in capitalising them and calculating depreciation: how would this improve accountability or performance measurement? The same applies even more to expenditure on art gallery and museum acquisitions and the like. The latest regulations (Home Office Voluntary Services Unit 1995) recognise the difficulty of the usual capital/revenue distinctions in charities by requiring charities, whose gross income in any year exceeds £100,000 and who cannot choose simply a receipts and payments basis, to produce a statement of financial activities focusing on analysis of all incoming resources and the application of resources. It is a wider-ranging statement than the income and expenditure account which was formerly required.

Nor is it certain that charities, formed for a specific purpose, should automatically expect to be going concerns for the foreseeable future. It is generally assumed that investors in a business will seek to perpetuate the profit-earning capability of the business. But there is no need for such an assumption in a not-for-profit activity.

On the other hand, there are concepts applicable in charities which are not generally applicable to businesses. In particular, charity accounts must account for the requirements of trust law in respecting the wishes of the donors by using the concept of *fund accounting*. In cases where donors have provided money to be held permanently for the benefit of the charity, this should be separately held as an endowment fund, the capital of which is not available for distribution to beneficiaries, though the income from endowment fund investments will be. Some donors may provide donations for purposes within the general objects of the charity but which they specifically limit to certain narrower objects. These are restricted funds, each of which must be kept in a separate fund account and not mixed with the general funds of the charity. Even the general funds may be subdivided to recognise designated funds earmarked by the trustees for specific future needs.

Annual accounts are mainly produced for purposes of accountability; in business they are the way the managers of the organisation must account to its owners. In a not-for-profit enterprise it seems doubtful whether the preparation of accounts on commercial principles is helpful. Certainly cash-based accounting is more certain and less open to manipulation. Naturally, management needs much more information than receipts and payments to manage its business – both forward-looking as well as backward-looking information – but that is a separate matter and one of management information rather than accountability.

Fortunately, the deregulation task force which has recently been considering accounting requirements for charities has allowed charities with an annual income of less than £100,000 to prepare cash-based accounts; this replaced the previously recommended limit of £25,000.

A further aspect of charity activity which may be mentioned here is the fact that income segmentation is so important, not only by type of donor as we will discuss later, but also by the form in which income is received for tax purposes. The regulations relating to tax relief on gifts are complex and frequently amended, which means that procedures must be in place to ensure that regulations are complied with and any tax reclaimable is promptly claimed.

The public sector

The public sector, just like charities, is also not normally subjected to the disciplines of the marketplace – the corporate finance market and the consumer price market – which together ensure efficiency.

Over the last decade, however, the public sector has been exposed to measures to bring the commercial disciplines of the market to bear. The government's Financial Management Initiative, launched in 1982, started the process and introduced the value-for-money concepts of efficiency, economy and effectiveness – the three Es – which we will consider later. The White Paper (House of Commons Treasury and Civil Service Committee 1982) raised the issues of organisation and management delegation when it sought

to promote in each department an organisation and system in which managers at all levels have:
a. a clear view of their objectives, and means to assess and, wherever possible, measure outputs and performance in relation to those objectives;
b. well defined responsibility for making the best use of their resources, including a critical scrutiny of output and value for money; and

c. the information (particularly about costs), the training and the access
    to expert advice that they need to exercise their responsibilities
    effectively.

The Thatcher government which launched the Initiative was responsible for taking many public sector bodies directly into the
private, market, sector by way of privatisation, making such
bodies subject to the disciplines of both the corporate finance and
the trading cycles. Within the public sector, the 'Next Steps' programme launched in 1988 set out to reorganise central government to take greater account of the needs of customers. Executive
functions were increasingly transferred to agencies headed by
chief executives with defined tasks and budgets. NHS reforms
were designed to separate the role of customer and provider, to
allow negotiated contracts of service and make managers responsible for performance against specified standards. *Competing for
Quality* (HM Treasury 1991) continued the process of introducing
service contracts and service level agreements which defined
standards of performance and responsibility for achieving them;
departments and executive agencies had to publish annual targets for market testing, local authority compulsory competitive
tendering was extended, and health authorities and trusts had to
report on market-testing plans. This was within the context of the
Citizen's Charter, which aimed to improve government services
by greater customer focus and making public services more responsive to the wishes of their users.

  Most recently, a consultation paper, *Better Accounting for the
Taxpayer's Money: Resource Accounting and Budgeting in Government* (HM Treasury 1994) was issued. The foreword to the paper
describes the proposed changes as

probably the most important reform of Civil Service accounting and
budgeting arrangements this century. . . . Resource accounting will enable managers in departments to evaluate the cost of using capital and
current resources on an equivalent basis . . . it will also provide a much
better means than we have had for setting departmental objectives and
outputs in terms of resources used. Taxpayers will be better able to see
what they are receiving for their money and to judge what value for
money they are getting.

  At the same time as these reforms are going on internally, central government bodies are usually within the audit arrangements

of the National Audit Office and local government bodies within the ambit of the Audit Commission. Both ensure that their public sector audits are subject to value-for-money review and public report in a way not generally applicable to the charity sector.

In many ways the public sector arrangements for performance review and accountability, which would have been considered rather rudimentary a decade or so ago, have gone beyond the standards set in the private sector. The charity sector could learn some useful lessons from developments in the public sector, and some of these will be identified in subsequent chapters.

Finally, it is worth considering the views of the National Council for Voluntary Organisations (NCVO), whose working party on effectiveness in the sector reported in 1990 that

> if an organisation is seeking to improve its efficiency and effectiveness, it should look at its own internal flow of management information. Voluntary organisations have been slow to adopt the standard tools of management which are used widely in the commercial, and increasingly in the public, sectors. . . . In many charities, the priority put on good financial management comes a very poor second to the implementation of the organisation's charitable objects. But the two need to go together since, unless charities operate with the same degree of financial rigour as commercial organisations, they will not effectively utilise the funds which are put at their disposal.
>
> (NCVO 1990)

Conclusions and key points

Charities differ from both private sector and public sector bodies in the degree to which they must demonstrate that they provide value for money.

Private sector businesses operating in the marketplace must satisfy customers as to value for money in order to continue trading and avoid losses; in the long run they must also satisfy their investors through corporate financial strategies if they are to continue and grow. Inefficient businesses cannot survive indefinitely in a competitive market, as demonstrated during the last recession by the record levels of corporate failure in 1991/92.

The public not-for-profit sector does not have to satisfy customers in price terms, nor does its funding depend on earning a return on capital. However, during the 1980s and 1990s it has been subjected to market-type disciplines. Much of the public sector has been transferred to the private sector, of course, and what remains has been influenced by measures which mimic market forces. Moreover, public sector bodies are usually subject to audits and value-for-money reviews which are publicly debated.

Some of these measures are having an effect on the voluntary sector through the contracting for services which might previously have been funded by grant aid. Accounting standards – originally developed to make businesses more accountable for commercial activities and specifically to measure annual profits or losses for shareholders – are being applied to a greater extent to not-for-profit organisations.

Accountants claim that the more commercial accounting practices make charities more accountable and are designed to show the true use of resources expended in any period. So-called resource accounting places a burden on charities' administration, however, and makes accounts more open to judgement and the possibility of creative accounting practices compared with the certainty of cash accounting. Fortunately, the latest regulations allow smaller charities to present accounts prepared on a cash basis.

Audited accounts are backward-looking by their nature. They are intended to serve the interests of accountability. Management needs to have forward-looking information. In this management context past accounts are relevant only for reviewing what has happened and for setting future plans within trends and previous experience.

Many of the arguments about accountability in the charity sector seem to confuse these roles. Trustees and managers ought to require a great deal of information for planning and decision-making purposes, much of which is referred to in this book, but there seems no need for all this to be contained in annual reports produced historically to account for the use of trust funds by trustees.

The NCVO has concluded that in the recent and prolonged debate about the need to improve financial management in charities, there has been great emphasis on external accountability and relatively little discussion on how to improve internal management information. In particular, it has recommended management tools such as strategic plans, annual budgets, regular management information reporting variances between actual and budget, and the production of a mission statement. Some of these matters are considered in the chapters which follow.

3 Getting a handle on performance: a value-for-money framework

> One of the most basic differences between non-profit organisations and businesses is that the typical non-profit has so many more relationships that are vitally important. In all but the very biggest businesses, the key relationships are fewer – employees, customers, and owners, and that's it. Every non-profit organisation has a multitude of constituencies and has to work out the relationship with each of them.
>
> Peter Drucker, *Managing the Non-profit Organisation*, Oxford, 1990, as quoted by Bruce 1993)

Return on capital employed

We have seen in the previous chapter that there is no corporate finance cycle in a charity. The theory of corporate finance depends on the concept that investors seek to maximise their return on investment, so far as this is consistent with the risk. This gives a fundamental justification for businesses and ultimately allows business activities to be measured and prioritised by reference to their effect on the profitability of the business as a whole.

For the business financial manager, this means a dual role of seeking, on the one hand, sources of finance which have the lowest cost of capital for the firm, and, on the other hand, to invest the finance in business activities which will produce the highest return.

Performance can be judged, principally, by reference to a measure of profitability – that is, to profit earned relative to the amount invested or the return on capital employed. The return on capital for the business as a whole can be subdivided between that applicable to shareholders, when it may be better expressed as a price/earnings ratio, and that applicable to the bankers or other sources of borrowings.

Similarly, the overall return on capital can be explained in terms of profit margin and capital utilisation ratios since profit/capital (return on capital) = profit/sales (profit margin) × sales/capital (capital utilisation ratio). The subsidiary ratios may be further subdivided in order to analyse the return on capital employed in whatever level of detail is required. These relationships are often referred to as the *pyramid of ratios* (Figure 3.1).

It is true that there are minor difficulties in defining some of these terms exactly, just as there are problems in the accounting calculations of profit and capital employed. And there is room for debate about how to apply short-term measures of profit to assess performance in the long run. Even so, the concept of profitability is unassailable as the key measure of corporate performance and a vast service industry exists to analyse, compare and communicate, through stockbrokers, merchant bankers, business media and a variety of financial advisers, what returns are earned by companies and to advise on investment in companies.

The concept of return on capital cannot be applied to a charity which does not exist for profit-making purposes (though it may be very relevant to trading subsidiaries which are formed to produce profits for the benefit of the charity). In particular, there is normally no meaningful 'sales' figure in a charity, because services are not usually sold commercially. Indeed, charities often exist because their 'customers' cannot afford to buy the services which they need at an economic price. Without a commercial sales value it is not possible to arrive at a profit or value-added figure.

In the absence of return on capital there is sometimes a temptation to seek some other charity performance indicator which will express success in a single figure – some prime ratio to which other performance measures could be linked in a quantifiable framework like the pyramid of ratios. Argenti (1993) suggests that

every organisation . . . should set out to benefit one clearly defined group of beneficiaries, and that a single, long term, verifiable, target figure should be set to reflect what it is trying to do for them. If it cannot set such a target it should be re-formed until this becomes possible.

It would be ideal if such a single figure could be found but how, for example, would this figure be determined for the Royal

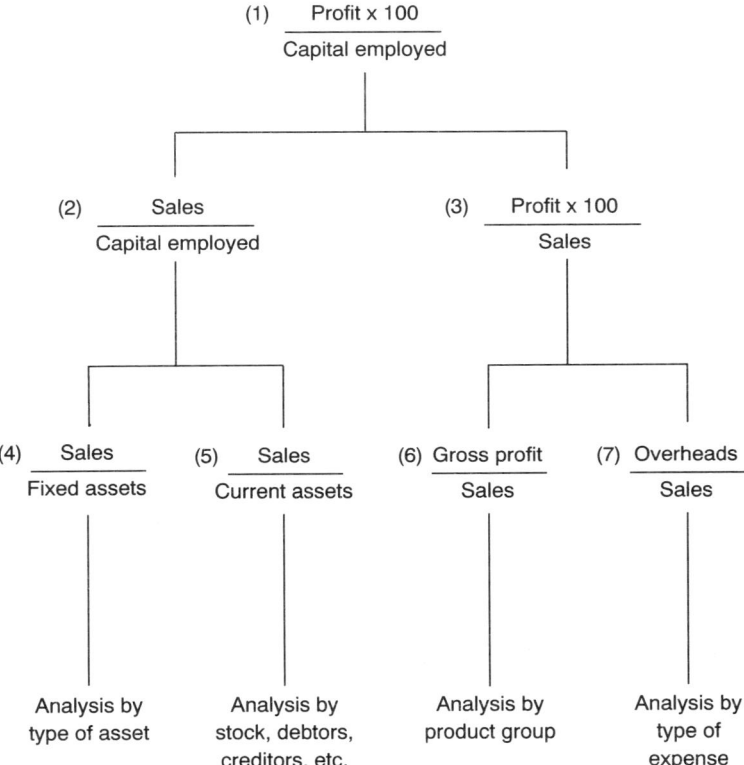

Note: Ratio 1, return on capital employed, equals ratio 2, capital utilisation, multiplied by ratio 3, profit margin.
Ratio 2 equals ratio 4 plus ratio 5, when these are best expressed more specifically in terms such as 'sales per square foot' or 'days credit outstanding', for example.
Ratio 3 equals ratio 6 minus ratio 7.

Figure 3.1 The pyramid of ratios

National Life-boat Institution, the Samaritans, the Royal Society for the Protection of Birds (RSPB) or the Salvation Army? There is no doubt that clarity of objectives and greater focus would be beneficial to the management of many charities, but it seems unlikely that it would be possible or even desirable to summarise charity performance in a single figure.

This is partly because there is no common language, as there is in the case of finance, to translate achievements in charities. Business sales can all be expressed in money values and compared with other values. The work of the RNLI can be costed, but the value of the work would be difficult to calculate. If it were calculated, it would make little sense to compare it with the value of the work done by the RSPB, and comparisons of value could hardly be made in a meaningful way. There is no common denominator for the value of benefits produced by each organisation nor a rate of exchange between them.

Value-for-money analysis

Performance is too complex to be reduced to a single indicator, especially, in charities, to a financial indicator. The complex concept of value for money may be simplified by breaking it down into three aspects: economy, efficiency and effectiveness, already introduced as the three Es. Economy implies minimal expenditure consistent with the aims; efficiency implies the relationship of outputs to inputs or productivity; and effectiveness implies the relationship between outputs and aims. These factors can be related to each other, as Figure 3.2 illustrates.

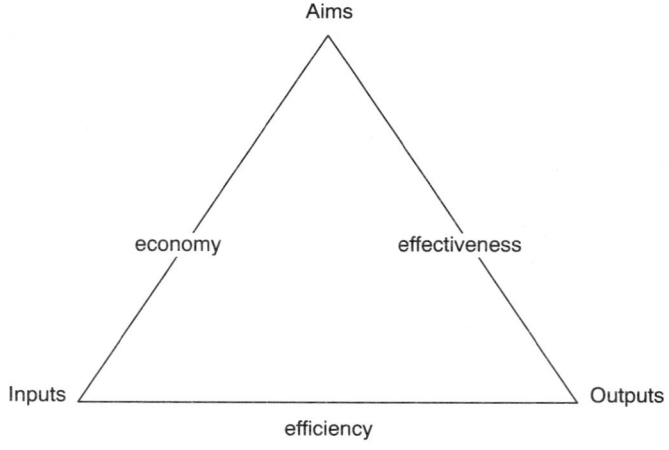

Figure 3.2 Value for money and the three Es

In a commercial business the main element is that of efficiency: the difference between cost inputs and revenue outputs, which represents profit and which is itself a principal aim. Profitability is both a measure of efficiency (profit output compared with capital input) but also an end in itself and thus a measure of effectiveness. But public services, even if required to break even or to earn a return on capital, usually have to place emphasis on effectiveness above efficiency since they frequently serve national economic or social ends, whose results are likely to take precedence over mere financial surplus. The efficiency of airport operations is important, but the public will forgive some lack of efficiency if operations are effective in preventing air collisions and terrorist activities, for example. And even in the private sector the profit motive of shareholders is modified increasingly by the interests of the community at large, so some authorities have added to the three Es those of ethics, environment and equity (see Open University 1993, for example). But I believe that ethical, environmental and equitable concerns are all part and parcel of the aims of the charity and that the simple value-for-money triangle helps to analyse and clarify the question of performance measurement.

We have already referred to the lack of market disciplines in the charity sector. The nature of the sector itself is also likely to impact unfavourably on value for money. Friedman (1980) classifies spending under four cases depending on whether you are spending your own money or someone else's, and whether you are spending for your own benefit or for the benefit of someone else. If you spend your own money on yourself you are concerned with economy, efficiency and effectiveness. If you are spending your own money on someone else, as when buying a present, you are concerned with economy but less with efficiency (as one's useless presents received often testify). If you are spending someone else's money on yourself, as with an expense account lunch, you do not worry too much about economy but you are going to ensure effectiveness and to get your money's worth. If you are spending someone else's money on someone else, then you have no direct motivation to seek economy, efficiency or effectiveness.

Trustees of charities are, of course, in the latter position. As Friedman (1980) says of bureaucrats in relation to welfare state programmes, they spend someone else's money on someone else. Only human kindness, not the much stronger and more dependable spur of self-interest, assures that they will spend the money in the way most beneficial to the recipients. Hence the wastefulness and ineffectiveness of the spending.

Trustees have a legal duty to operate the trust properly and no doubt most trustees act responsibly – but they have no material motive to achieve value for money, indeed they are prohibited generally from receiving any financial reward for carrying out their duties as trustees. Failures in providing value for money frequently arise and spectacular failures are reported in the press from time to time.

For these reasons charities need to put disciplines and systems in place to safeguard the interests of the beneficiaries who can usually exert little power over the way money is spent by charities.

Controlling efficiency is relatively easy compared with controlling effectiveness since charities frequently have aims which are complex, not easily expressed in money values, and difficult to quantify. Even so, it would be wrong to concentrate on economy and efficiency just because these concepts are easier to control than effectiveness. The latter is more important because it goes to the heart of the question about what a charity is and whether it is discharging its purpose well. For example, the National Audit Office investigation of the Overseas Development Administration (ODA) was reported by *Third Sector* ('Tighter checks for overseas aid', 18 November 1993) as follows:

The ODA contributed £10 million towards the Simple Truth appeal for Kurdish refugees through the British Red Cross and the UN, but failed to carry out an assessment of the impact of the aid. . . . The report recommends that in future all organisations receiving funds should, in addition to a financial report, produce a three or four page report describing the aid and the use it was put to, and detailing any problems or lessons to be learned.

Argenti (1993) expresses the need to control effectiveness strongly when he writes:

I want to know, not just in words but with figures, what each socially significant organisation thinks it is doing for whom and how well it is doing it . . . if an organisation cannot express its aims numerically then there is something fundamentally wrong with its aims, so much so that it cannot be considered a viable entity in the modern world.

The idea of tackling performance measurement by looking separately at the three elements of economy, efficiency and effectiveness has been well tried in the public sector and forms the basis of much value-for-money audit work. It should be applied more purposefully to charitable organisations and is considered in more depth in subsequent chapters.

Ratio analysis

Having outlined the elements of value for money in terms of efficiency, economy and effectiveness, it will be appreciated that each of these measures is derived from two aspects. Economy implies a relationship between aims and inputs, efficiency between inputs and outputs, effectiveness between outputs and aims (see Figure 3.2).

Ratios are a simple way of expressing the relationship between two figures as one figure, in the form of a fraction, a percentage or a simple ratio. The pyramid of ratios considered earlier consists of financial ratios – but ratios may be non-financial (such as hours worked per volunteer), or partly financial and non-financial (such as takings per shop customer).

We use ratios all the time for understanding and control. When driving a car, for example, it is normal to keep an eye on the ratio of distance to time (miles per hour) in order to judge speed. Similarly, the ratio of distance to fuel used (miles per gallon) is used as the principal indicator of efficiency. In this case the ratio is non-financial but it is used to help us to make a financial judgement, since petrol usage is a major element of motoring costs.

Absolute figures alone tell us very little. It is only when they are compared with one another that they can be judged to be good or bad, improvement or deterioration. Performance measures to be developed are usually, therefore, in the form of ratios. In a business situation many of the key indicators are financial indicators; in a charity it is to be expected that many indicators will be non-financial and particular to the charity under consideration. Exactly which ratios are important will depend on what element of value for money is under consideration and on the perspective of the person seeking information.

It should also be remembered that measuring value for money, as in measuring anything, involves some imprecision. The science of measurement requires that large, complex phenomena be simplified to objective, operational and measurable dimensions. Any performance measure is in this way something less than the performance itself, which is why the measurement of performance is a matter of important judgement for trustees and managers.

Some authorities make a distinction between performance *measures*, indicating precise and unambiguous figures, and performance *indicators*, which are less definitive and merely suggestive of conclusions. For example, a higher ratio of miles per gallon suggests that a car is more economic to run, but this is not conclusive evidence; the ratio is merely an indicator. Some quality cars with high petrol consumption have been shown to be economic because they last longer, have a higher resale value and lower depreciation. In this book I do not make a distinction between performance measures and performance indicators, since in my experience most measures are inevitably not absolutely precise and require sensible interpretation in the light of whatever other evidence may be available.

Stakeholder perspectives

Another reason why performance measurement is more problematical in charities than in businesses is the greater variety of the stakeholders. Businesses exist for the benefit of their shareholders. Charities exist for the benefit of the beneficiaries. But in both cases it is recognised that regard must be paid to other stakeholders if the primary stakeholder interests are to be best served.

Modern management writers suggest that there are five forces governing competition in an industry and that knowledge of these underlying sources of competitive pressure provides the groundwork for a strategic agenda for action (Porter 1979). These forces are: jockeying for position among current competitors; the threat of new entrants; the threat of new products; the bargaining position of suppliers; and the bargaining position of customers.

In commercial organisations the customer takes the product, thus demonstrating satisfaction with it, for a price which forms the main source of regular income for the organisation. In a charity the customer who receives the service frequently receives it free of charge or at a subsidised rate, while regular income is derived from grants or donations of various kinds. As Dr Diana Leat (1993) observes, 'to achieve its goals the voluntary organisation must serve the consumer but to survive it only needs to please the donor/funder'. I suggest, therefore, that there are six forces in a charitable situation rather than five. The customer as end-user of the service remains but in addition there is the customer (donor, grantor or testator) in the form of the provider of funds to supply the services; these persons are generally the same in a normal business trading situation, but are usually different in a charity.

In most charities, the customer as end-user of the service is usually unable to exercise much power, since as a beneficiary he/she is normally in an underprivileged and economically weak position. The 'customer' who provides income, on the other hand, is potentially in a strong position. This is particularly so when the donor is a central government department or local authority. Maintaining good relations and good intelligence communications with such authorities is of great strategic significance to many charities.

The donor, whose funds allow the charity to function, may not always exert direct influence. But the type of donor on whom the organisation relies will affect the strategic stance of the charity, depending on whether the donor is the general public, the government, a grant-making trust or an endowment trust. For example, the trustees of Guide Dogs for the Blind, which is well able to attract substantial funds from the general public, may be able to adopt a strategy different from that of less popular aids- or drug-related charities, which are generally obliged to depend on short-term government core funding.

Suppliers of labour, especially the volunteers delivering the service, have much potential power, even though they are not organised or economically motivated to exploit that power.

The threat of new entrants or substitute products is not strong in charities but the political climate in the UK does not favour monopoly suppliers and encourages competition. This may be seen as a potential threat to be kept in view by large charities reliant on government funding, though the threat may be countered by demonstrating to offer good value for money.

More recently management writers have emphasised the importance of long-term relationships between stakeholders, perhaps taking into account the success of Japanese consensus management culture, which they have referred to as corporate architecture. Architecture in this sense means the links between a company, its employees, customers and suppliers, which provide a foundation of institutional knowledge and adaptability. A network of stable relational contracts or implicit understanding between participants is the basis of strong architecture. Such contracts flourish over a long period of time because players' knowledge that they must go on dealing with each other discourages selfish opportunism and favours a mutually beneficial outcome. 'Architecture does not create extraordinary organisations by assembling extraordinary people . . . but by enabling ordinary people to perform in extraordinary ways' (Kaye 1993). This expresses well the way in which charities have been able to utilise the goodwill of many ordinary volunteers and commercial companies, not always with government backing or with any economic motivation, to obtain social or philanthropic benefits.

The beneficiaries of a charity are *de jure* the most important stakeholders since it is for them that the charity was formed and continues to exist. But the beneficiaries are usually, often inevitably, unable to exert any real power. They may have to rely on unpaid trustees who are not necessarily in executive positions. It is the managers of the charity who *de facto* exercise the greatest power. Argenti (1974) went to some length to differentiate *de jure* from *de facto* control and observed somewhat cynically 'that the purpose of any organisation is whatever is decided by those who have power to decide it'.

The first step towards controlling value for money and providing a framework for performance measurement is therefore to clarify the purpose and objectives of the organisation, which is the subject of the next chapter.

Conclusions and key points

The overall purpose of a business is to make a proper return on its capital employed, and most business ratios can be related to this primary ratio. Charities do not have such a common aim and without it there is no single ratio which can be used to encapsulate overall performance or to compare the performance of one charity with that of another.

Assessing performance in a charity is a complex task requiring consideration of both financial and non-financial results. Assessment is best made by separate consideration of the three Es – economy, efficiency and effectiveness – where economy denotes providing resources at the least cost consistent with the objectives; efficiency means maximising outputs relative to resources; and effectiveness measures the degree to which outputs achieve the results intended. In an organisation seeking to maximise profitability, efficiency must be the principal concern; charities, by their nature, pursue ends which do not have a direct economic payback, and for them effectiveness should be the principal concern.

The concepts of value for money – the three Es – imply a comparison or relationship between two factors. Performance indicators should reflect this by being in the form of ratios of some sort. They may be financial (such as direct expenditure on charitable objects as a proportion of income received) or non-financial (such as the proportion of hostel bed spaces occupied); both these examples are input/output ratios indicating efficiency.

It is helpful also to consider performance measurement from the perspective of the various stakeholders concerned. Argenti (1993) has little patience with modern theories of reconciling stakeholders' interests and holds that charities should be for the beneficiaries, whose interests must be paramount. Beneficiaries of charities require special consideration because they are usually unable to exercise any power and there is always a danger that their interests will be subordinated to those with more power in the organisation. At the same time, the donors who make the operations of the charity possible must also be considered, for their wishes establish the trust funds and must be respected to avoid any breach of trust.

4 The vision thing: mission, means and measures

> All this urges people in or related to organisations to dream constructively, to project their ambitions for service boldly, without prejudging the external support that those dreams and ambitions could generate. There is the heart and the centre of energy for the charity.
>
> (Mullin 1995)

In the value for money diagram in the previous chapter (Figure 3.2), the top of the triangle was labelled 'Aims'. This is because establishing aims and objectives is the starting point for operational performance measurement. As was argued in Chapter 1, establishing some consensus about objectives is essential as a foundation for rational decision-making in any organisation.

Mission

This is less true of businesses, where the ultimate purpose can be assumed to be the generation of profit, than for charities. Indeed, it is easy to be cynical about corporate mission statements, which tend to promise all things to all men, and to feel some sympathy with the Yorkshire company which was quoted as announcing that 'grit and gumption are preferable to inertia and intellect'. Some of the most successful companies, such as Marks and Spencer, do not have a formal mission statement. But perhaps this is because they have been so successful in projecting their corporate image without one. Even so, most companies now put their values down on paper in a mission statement of some sort. Quite why this transatlantic trend has become so fashionable is difficult to say, but it seems to fit in with the need to make lower levels of management more responsive and responsible. The modern management practices of greater delegation, flatter organisation structures, employee empowerment, and the ability to thrive in a climate of change, all depend on employees having an understanding of strategic aims and common values. This is even more important for non-profit-making organisations since they do not have the profit motive, which tends to foster goal congruence and provides a ready means of prioritising and comparing alternative action plans.

It should be easier for charities to establish a mission statement because a charity by definition must subscribe to certain charitable objects which will be set out in the charity's constitution. This tends to be a legal statement, however, whereas a good mission statement has been said to 'lift the heart and concentrate the mind' – qualities which legal objects clauses usually fail to capture effectively. For example, the Salvation Army International Trust Trustee's Report quotes the aims as

to further the work of the Salvation Army in any part of the world and in particular the work of International Headquarters of the Army and otherwise in furtherance of the objects of the Army as set out in section 3 of the Salvation Army Act 1980 namely the advancement of the Christian religion as promulgated in the religious doctrines set in Schedule 1 to the Act.

The mission statement, on the other hand, starts in a much more uplifting way by declaring:

The International Headquarters of The Salvation Army acts . . . to affirm that The Salvation Army, an evangelical part of the universal Christian Church, is motivated by love for God and its mission is to preach the gospel of Jesus Christ and meet human need in his name without discrimination . . .

The mission statement serves the organisation on a number of levels. Of course it is a statement about strategic aims, but it is also the start of a communication process, whereby plans agreed at senior level are translated into action plans and budgets, through which individuals can be aligned with the organisation and their efforts focused on agreed priorities.

This process of translation of a vision through the overall mission statement and a statement of corporate values to departmental and ultimately individual objectives has been referred to as the *objectives cascade*, and is illustrated in Figure 4.1. The individual is shown at the end of the top-down cascade process. But the cascade also allows training and staff/volunteer development needs to be identified and provides feedback from individuals into the objective setting processes. And it is essential, especially in a voluntary organisation, that the establishment of the mission should be reached through a consultative process which can be owned by all those involved.

Not all organisations will distinguish these steps in the same way. A vision implies a view of a future state of affairs which is better than that which exists. The mission suggests strategic action to be taken to realise or move towards the vision. But the terms are not used in a precise way and precise definitions are perhaps not very important.

In *Investing in People – VSO's Strategic Plan for the 1990s*, VSO sets out its purpose, values and distinctive features. Its purpose is succinctly stated as follows: 'VSO enables men and women to

Figure 4.1 The objectives cascade

work alongside people in poorer countries in order to share skills, build capabilities and promote international understanding and action, in the pursuit of a more equitable world'. So, a more equitable world is the VSO vision and its mission is well expressed in its statement of purpose. The document goes on to state that VSO:

- values the individual and believes in the equal right of all to realise their potential
- believes in countering disadvantage by practical action, person to person
- values action motivated by and responding to the needs of others, both through work abroad and through voluntary activity by supporters at home
- values and respects diversity of culture
- values two-way partnership which openly shares costs and benefits
- values the learning and friendship which results from people living and working alongside each other in pursuit of shared goals.

These statements of purpose and values are a useful start to the strategic plans of the VSO, an organisation which works to achieve its purpose through volunteers, who must accept the values of the organisation if they are to be effective in it.

The World Wildlife Fund for Nature, WWF UK, stated its vision as

to be influential and publicly trusted, working for the conservation of nature and ecological processes in line with WWF's international mission; in collaboration with key partners inside and outside the WWF family, to address the most pressing, as well as the long-term global and local environmental problems which affect biological diversity worldwide; to have a reputation as an organisation that gets things done.

The American Red Cross, another organisation which relies on volunteers, when seeking in 1988 to redefine its aims and working methods, produced a report which stated:

The mission of the American Red Cross is to improve the quality of human life; to enhance self-reliance and to help people avoid, prepare for, and cope with emergencies. It does this through services that are governed and directed by volunteers and are consistent with its congressional charter and the principles of the International Red Cross which are stated as humanity, impartiality, neutrality, independence, voluntary service, unity and universality.

(quoted by Presland, n.d.)

The Royal Society for the Protection of Birds, in its publication *Future Directions – The RSPB Corporate Strategy 1992/97*, expresses its vision as follows:

We aim to be the foremost bird conservation organisation, as well as having considerable expertise and understanding in broader nature conservation and environmental policy. Birds will continue to be the foundation of our work. Given their visibility, popularity and value as indicator species for the health of the whole environment, birds provide an excellent focus for a wide range of conservation work. We believe the RSPB will achieve most for conservation by keeping wild birds at the core of its mission while developing our work on broader conservation and environmental issues. Our commitment is to all wild birds and the wider countryside, though we will continue to concentrate on priority species and habitats in order to use our resources most effectively. As an organisation, we aim for good working relationships with our members and other organisations and effectiveness in organising the Society's work.

Some of the examples above are rather wordy but they all illustrate the importance, especially when volunteers are involved, in starting from a position of a set of values which have the effect of reinforcing the identity of the organisation, establishing a framework for priorities, maintaining staff and volunteer loyalty and presenting a clear image to the outside world.

Rankin (n.d.) claims that the case for a mission statement,

the development of values which inform that statement and the working out of practice based on those values rests on two issues. First, the need for volunteer using organisations to anchor their policies and strategies within their own terms of reference and thus make them less vulnerable to external pressures and to losing control over the direction they choose to go in. Second, the need to ensure real volunteer satisfaction which can only be achieved if volunteers feel a genuine ownership of the process. . . . A value system for volunteer using organisations is important as a way of safeguarding the interests of volunteers and determining what they do and why they do it. A value system which is not rooted in a mission statement remains at the theoretical level and has little long term practical effect on practice.

He contrasts this value-based approach to a utilitarian, task-based approach which he says

nearly always results in attaching great importance to organisational matters and, in the end, the organisation and its own interests become a value in themselves rather than remaining the means of achieving the original value which was the accomplishment of the task.

The previous paragraphs have suggested that it is necessary to step back from the aims of the organisation and to establish first the mission and values as a prerequisite to defining the aims. They also suggest that a charity should always keep the interests of its beneficiaries firmly in mind lest the interests of the organisational players, with *de facto* power, take precedence over the beneficiaries, with only *de jure* power.

A strategic and operational performance measurement model

The value-for-money triangle (Figure 3.2), which seems to me to be a good model for considering operational performance, should perhaps be extended into a figure-of-eight model, where the operational performance cycle (aims–inputs–process–outputs) is fed by a strategic performance cycle (needs recognition–vision–aims–operations–outcomes). This model (shown in Figure 4.2) recognises the importance of vision, through the mission and values statement, in establishing aims and objectives. It also shows the importance of recognising and

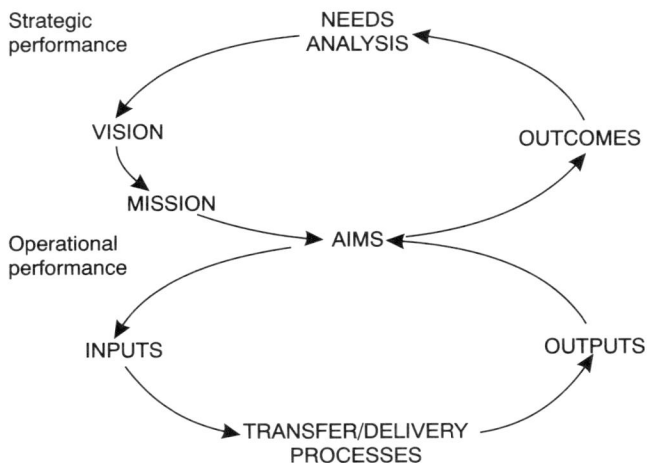

Figure 4.2 Figure-of-eight model for value for money

reviewing the needs of the beneficiaries in informing the vision and evaluating feedback from results. Finally, it recognises that outcomes are, as we will see later, sometimes rather remote from outputs but that outcomes are of importance in the evaluation of strategic performance.

Means

Mission statements are inevitably worded in a general, even idealistic, manner. They are not themselves useful for assessing performance until they have been subdivided into manageable elements and extended into measurable aims and objectives.

Sometimes the long-term mission has to be approached indirectly by subsidiary objectives. For example, a major international charity with a mission to reduce Third World poverty felt that a prime way to reduce poverty would be to improve education. Improving education in parts of Africa was hindered by the fact that during the dry season mothers and children had to spend days in trekking to collect water. Consequently, operational objectives were to install effective water supplies as a necessary step in the strategy of better education which in turn would assist the mission of the relief of poverty.

In subdividing the mission it is common to identify what may be termed *critical success factors* or *key performance areas* – aspects of performance considered vital to the achievement of the overall mission.

The VSO strategic plan, for example, refers, under the heading 'Key Directions', to its intention to pursue three main thrusts over the next five years. The first, 'Extend and Enhance the Two-year Programme', is made up of four main actions; the second, 'Offer New Services to Overseas Partners', refers to three significant themes; while the third, 'Raise Awareness of Development Issues and Change Public Attitudes', contains three action programmes.

WWF UK recognised six key themes which would contribute to its vision:

• promoting fundamental change in environmental behaviour;
• direct intervention to protect endangered species or ecological systems;

- key partnerships;
- fund gathering;
- effective operations;
- the organisation, its people and environment.

Each key theme is further analysed into about half a dozen generic strategies. Thus, the key theme of promoting fundamental change in environmental behaviour contains six generic strategies:

- promote sustainable development practices linking conservation with human needs;
- promote the establishment and implementation of international treaties and national policies;
- reduce consumption and pollution and their effects on nature by influencing public policy and the practices of consumers, business and industry;
- promote environmental education and building capacity to enable people to manage their own natural resources;
- create and maintain effective and sustainable systems of protected areas; and
- protect species of special concern.

The RSPB strategy document, referred to previously, proceeds to outline priorities under the headings of conservation priorities, conservation action, international conservation, working with our members, spreading the word, values, the staff team and resources.

The Victoria and Albert Museum mission statement says: 'The Museum exists to increase the understanding and enjoyment of art, craft and design through its collections.' This is a nice, succinct statement, and it is followed by a recognition of the four primary objectives which the V&A pursues:

- to care for, preserve and add to the collection
- to ensure that the collections are made available to the public, both by display and by provision of reference facilities
- to add to the body of knowledge relevant to the collections through research
- to disseminate that knowledge.

(V & A Corporate Plan 1994–1998)

Measures

General statements are no use as objectives for use in performance measurement. A charity report recently sent to me says
that the objective of the company 'is advancement of the education of the public in the development of the piano and kindred
musical instruments'. This statement clearly requires further
work before it can be used to establish any measure of
performance.

Translating the broad mission statements and key themes into
quantifiable objectives with appropriate performance measures is
an essential step to planning and controlling action. The management saying 'What gets measured gets done' expresses the importance of measurement in the management of results and in the
motivation of those involved.

Broad objectives will have been agreed by the senior management team and cascaded down the management chain by way of
key themes to a sufficiently low level at which individuals are able
to link their personal objectives to those of the organisation. At this
lower level, objectives should be quantifiable. It is sometimes said
that they should be *smart*, a mnemonic whose letters stand for
*s*pecific, *m*easurable, *a*chievable, *r*elevant and *t*ime-related.

Objectives at operational management level must be specific in
their relationship to the manager concerned; they are subsets of
higher-level objectives but specific in relation to the individual
manager for whom they are set. They must be measurable; it is
difficult to imagine any meaningful or logical management process without measurement, though it is not always easy to define
good measures. Where objectives are related to client satisfaction,
for example, it may be necessary to set up sample survey processes. Generally, objectives should focus on achievements rather
than on processes.

It is clearly desirable that objectives should be achievable and
relevant. In striving for improvement it is to be expected that
targets should be ambitious and reflect a higher standard than
that previously achieved, but it would be cynical and self-
defeating to set targets at an impossibly high level. The objectives
set should be reached with the agreement of the individuals concerned and should be within their sphere of influence with whatever support is agreed to be provided by the organisation.

Objectives need to be time-related since time is an essential element of planning and control functions. Strategic objectives, by definition, tend to be related to long-term time-scales which may cover several years or even decades whereas, operational objectives may have very short time-scales relating to a project, work period or shift. The budget, however, is the principal planning and control document within the organisation and this implies that most objectives will be related to the budget period of a financial year.

The requirement that objectives should be expressed in quantified measurable terms, and the expectation that many of the objectives will be related to the financial year for budget purposes, does not mean that they will necessarily be expressed in financial terms. Lower management objectives are usually best quantified in physical measures of some sort, while it is more common for higher levels of objectives to be expressed, in part at least, in financial terms. There is sometimes some reluctance to quantify ethical and non-financial factors since it is often difficult to do so. This is really no excuse for failing to manage as effectively as possible and measures can usually be devised even in complex circumstances. The VSO vision of a more equitable world might be difficult to quantify, but it uses the Human Development Index of the United Nations Development Programme to indicate the national degree of inequity or need for support, an index based on three components: life expectancy at birth; educational attainment derived from adult literacy rate and years of schooling; and adjusted real gross domestic product. In this way a very complex concept is translated into a simple quantified and measurable figure which can be used for assessing and comparing needs and which could be used for assessing outcomes.

Action

The mission tells us where we want the organisation to go and the measures tell how we will know the extent to which we are progressing towards our goal. The means are the action plans which we will follow. They are programmes or projects designed to achieve the organisation's objectives, defined by quantified, recognisable, delivered results within defined time-scales, and including agreed responsibilities for the achievement of results.

The action plans will quantify the resources to be used in implementing the projects or programmes and thus link into the organisation's budgetary planning and financial control systems, which are considered in more detail later in Chapter 6. Meanwhile, in the next chapter we look in more detail at measures needed to appraise performance and some of the tools to be used.

In this chapter we have considered the importance of setting objectives – developing a mission for the organisation as a whole, dividing this into key area objectives, and then subdividing it into subsidiary and individual objectives. We have also seen that measures have to be formulated so that objectives can be used by management for planning and control and as a starting point for developing, from the range of options available, preferred action plans. These in turn have to be quantified in financial terms as budgets. The whole process involves the comparison of a desired state of affairs with an existing state of affairs and the design and implementation of actions to bridge the gap. This programme of managing change is conveniently summarised in the Systems Intervention Strategy method (Open University 1993, Unit 2), where steps in managing change are described as shown in Table 4.1.

Table 4.1 Managing change

Phase	Step	Answer to question
Diagnosis	1. Description	Where are you now?
	2. Identify objectives and constraints	Where do you want to be?
	3. Formulate measures for your objectives	How will you know when you get there?
Design	4. Generate a range of options	How can you get there?
	5. Model options selectively	What will it be like?
Implementation	6. Evaluate options against measures	Will you like it?
	7. Design implementation strategies	How can you carry it through?
	8. Carry through the planned changes	

Conclusions and key points

Performance may be assessed at both the strategic and the operational levels. Strategic performance may need a period of several years for proper assessment and feedback to the strategic planning processes; operational performance needs to be constantly monitored so that day to day control can be exercised.

Operational performance depends on the establishment of objectives. Objectives in turn are derived from a strategic view of what a charity should be doing to bring about the alleviation of needs which it has recognised. This strategic view is expressed as a mission statement or statement of purpose. The mission statement is derived from the legal objects of the charity, but is a management statement rather than a legal one.

The mission statement is ideally supported by a statement of values to which the charity and those who work with it subscribe. This assists in reinforcing goal congruence within the organisation and in maintaining motivation among volunteers.

The mission statement is usually a general strategic affirmation. To be useful for operational planning and control purposes, it has to be translated into quantified objectives – objectives which are specific, measurable, achievable, relevant and time-related. This translation process, through mission to means to measures, means that the overall mission needs to be broken down first into key performance areas or critical success factors vital to the achievement of the mission.

From the critical success factors it is possible to derive divisional or departmental objectives out of which action plans may be developed and quantified in financial terms as budgets for formal approval. Individual work programmes and objectives may be derived from the divisional objectives within agreed action plans and budgets. In this way the strategic aims of the organisation are converted through the objectives cascade into increasingly specific operational targets and budgets for control.

5 Economy, efficiency and effectiveness: the holy trinity of value for money

> A project manager was questioned closely by his management committee on the effectiveness of work done with alcoholics. The committee received the tart response 'if this project saves one alcoholic then it has been successful'.
>
> (NCVO 1981)

> Besides, begging is efficient charity, a benefit in cash not in kind. Asking for money on the street is one-stop welfare at the point of delivery.
>
> (Simon Jenkins 1994)

Introduction

In the previous chapter we saw how the formulation of measurable objectives is a final stage in strategic planning and the starting point for operational planning and control. In this chapter we will consider how operational performance, by using resource inputs and producing service outputs, is related to objectives, and also how outputs lead in turn to outcomes which fit into the concept of strategic performance.

Having agreed aims and the cascade of objectives following the management chain within the organisation, then it is necessary to establish a system to capture and quantify the inputs and outputs.

Inputs

Inputs in cost terms will naturally be captured by the accounting system, which will generally follow an accounting code classification according to the nature of the payment under headings such as salaries, light and heat, printing and stationery, and so on. In all but the smallest organisations it is also necessary to classify cost inputs by reference to the organisational or responsibility structure, typically including direct charitable projects, fund-raising, publications, administration, and so on, and distinguishing the various branches, where these exist, from head office departments.

The cost heading classification allows the accounting statements to be presented in the traditional way; the organisational classification is required for budgetary control purposes to show who is responsible for the use of the resources expended. In charities, the organisational analysis must be extended to ensure that funds whose use is restricted by the terms of the trust, are accounted for separately and are not confused with the general funds of the charity; indeed, where several restricted funds exist it will be necessary to keep each one separate if the amounts are material, as it will where the trustees have designated some of the general funds for some particular purpose.

In parallel with the financial accounting analyses, it is common for commercial businesses to have a cost accounting system which attaches costs to the units for sale, so that managers are aware of the cost of items produced for sale and can thus monitor product profitability and take the information into account in pricing and volume decisions. Charities do not usually expect to sell goods and services in a commercial manner, and it may be argued that a cost accounting system is less relevant for them. Nevertheless, cost per unit should show the resources used in supplying a unit of service and is an important indicator of efficiency. Of course, where an activity is carried out for commercial purposes it becomes essential to know the cost. Thus in a fund-raising department, if the costs of fund-raising exceed the income produced by the department, this would call the whole operation into question.

Charities have, in any case, to analyse their expenditure under broad activity headings, such as direct charitable expenditure, fund-raising expenses, and publicity expenses, in order to comply with professional accounting recommendations.

The value of expenditure is the main means of expressing inputs to an organisation, but physical measures are also useful and, where appropriate, systems to record quantities as well as values are required. Where resources are a limiting factor to the provision of services – bed spaces in a hostel or consultant time in a clinic, for example – recording the availability, cost and usage of such resources is especially important. In many charities – Voluntary Service Overseas is an example – a prime resource is the skill and labour of volunteers. Accounting recommendations require donated assets to be included in accounting statements at a value even though they were not purchased by the charity for value. The recommendations stop short of requiring donated labour (volunteers) to be accounted for in value terms. Where volunteers are a key resource, however, they are a most important input which needs to be quantified for performance measurement purposes. Deciding what inputs to measure is a management judgement, but those resources which represent a large proportion of spending, which carry risk of some sort or which sigificantly affect the ability to deliver outputs, are likely to require measurement.

'Inputs' is the term used to denote the resources used in the production of outputs. Input measures may be total or partial; thus the use of a measure in terms of miles per gallon to assess the performance of a car uses gallons of petrol as a cost indicator even though petrol is only a partial cost of motor expenses. Inputs must be quantifiable and measurable. In identifying input units it will be necessary to define rules for measurement; for example, if measuring the use of secretarial time in producing reports, rules will be needed on the treatment of relaxation and sickness breaks. It is also necessary to install procedures for measuring physical inputs, for example by counting, documenting, weighing, and so on. The detail required will depend on the significance of the inputs and the degree of control deemed appropriate.

The costing of services provided by charities is becoming of increasing importance, too, because of the changes in government support for charities which put greater emphasis on contractual payment for services rather than on grants.

Costing and contracting

It is not the aim of this book to provide a costing textbook, but at this point it seems appropriate to include some explanation of what is implied by referring to a costing system and of the meaning of some of the costing terminology which appears later.

Costing implies a consideration of the relationship between values and quantities. Financial statements are much more informative when combined with information on physical events, and the purpose of costing is to allow an understanding of the relationship between physical events and costs or values so as to improve management planning and control.

Financial information on a vehicle fleet is much more use to the transport manager if it is supported by costing information showing cost per vehicle and cost per mile. If the manager was responsible for stocks of fuel he would need to know not just the value of fuel purchased but also the quantities delivered, in hand and used so that he could check that fuel was being properly controlled, ensure that wastage was kept to a minimum, and determine a proper charge-out rate for fuel issued – always assuming, of course, that the costs of operating a sophisticated costing system are justified by the benefits.

Costing is a problem because resources are acquired in one form – labour hours, boxes of stationery, units of electricity and so on – but are used to produce services in another form, such as information packs for local authorities, counselling sessions for clients or Third World development projects. Relating the units of inputs to those of the outputs means that assumptions and judgements must be built into the cost control system.

When costs are incurred which can be attributed wholly to the unit of output to be costed – for example, if stationery is purchased specifically for producing information packs – then no difficulty arises. Such costs are called *direct costs*.

When costs are not directly related to an output unit – for example, the majority of administration costs – it is necessary to apportion such costs over the range of relevant units using an equitable basis or to allocate them as appears most appropriate. Such costs are termed *indirect costs*. Inevitably there is room for differences of opinion on how best to recover indirect costs from output units. Accounting procedures will need to be designed to distribute indirect costs to services or products in a fair and consistent way.

Different terminology is used to describe the relationship of costs to volume. Some costs are likely to change directly with the volume of a service provided – for example, if it decided to send twice as many information packs to local authorities it is likely that the cost of stationery used in the packs will also double. Such costs are called *variable* costs or *marginal* costs.

Other costs are not affected by changes in volume and remain the same. So, for example, the labour cost of researching and preparing the information to be included in the packs will not change no matter how many packs are printed. Such costs are called *fixed* costs.

An understanding of fixed and variable costs is vital for preparing budgets and forecasts. The theoretical clear differentiation between fixed and variable is not always clear in practice; most costs are fixed in the short term but variable in the long term, and there is a range of semi-fixed or semi-variable costs between the two extremes.

There is scope for expending a great deal of effort in analysing costs and in devising systems for the allocation of costs to services and products. Activity-based costing is a currently fashionable subject which deals with more precise ways of attributing indirect costs to outputs and which recognises that there may be more complex reasons for cost changes other than those associated with simple volume. However, most charities will not need to invest in complex costing systems since benefits may be insufficient to justify the costs.

On the other hand, the current trend towards contracting, whereby official funds given to charities are tied to specific deliveries of services rather than given by way of grants, may require detailed service costings to be produced. In negotiations between charities and government agencies both parties need to understand cost behaviour and to appreciate that prices for services must allow the charity provider not only to cover the direct and variable costs of providing the service but also a proper contribution towards the overheads.

Gutch (1992), investigating the greater experience of the United States in contracting service provision through charities, found that voluntary organisations had 'suffered greatly from underfunding, late payment, a squeeze on overheads and other financial difficulties'. He recommended, among other things, that:

- voluntary organisations should reflect the full cost of providing a particular service, including all relevant overheads and transaction costs, when negotiating to provide a service . . . The contribution of volunteers and charitable funds should be separately identified as added value.
- government should recognise that contracting with the voluntary sector is not necessarily a cheap option and that it is not in the longer-

term interests of the voluntary sector or the people it serves to under-fund contracts.

- contracts should be based on payment for outcomes rather than on line-by-line monitoring of inputs. Allowance should be made for the difficulty of achieving outcomes in many areas of human services. Measuring outcomes is still at a very early stage of development and is likely to require considerable investment of time and effort.
- central and local government should invest in the provision of inde-pendent technical advice for voluntary organisations in the legal, financial, management, and other aspects of contracting.
- management committees should encourage voluntary organisations to become more businesslike in their contract negotiations and costings.

In a contracting relationship both parties to the contract need to understand the cost structure. In the business world top-class buyers such as Marks and Spencer and Sainsbury are known for their attention to negotiating tough but fair terms with their sup-pliers. They want the most economic price but recognise that it is not in their interest to negotiate prices so low as to put their suppliers out of business. Not all local authorities have yet learned this lesson in their negotiations with charity suppliers.

Outputs

Outputs in charities are not as readily expressed in value terms as are the inputs. The services provided by charities are often pro-vided to beneficiaries who are unable to pay an economic price for the services. Outputs can rarely be measured readily by means of money values, and it is therefore that much more important to install procedures to measure as closely as possible the physical outputs. Fund-raising is one of the few charitable activities where outputs, in the form of funds generated, can be best measured in money-value terms (and even here caution is required since many years can elapse between efforts to attract legacy income and the actual receipt of legacies; legacy income is a measure of a charity's efforts several years ago but not necessarily of today's).

Where outputs are events which can be counted with a fair degree of certainty the collection of output statistics is relatively easy, so a charity for helping children with no homes to find foster or adoptive parents will easily record the number of children linked to new parents. By analysing the figures to show how many children are linked within, say, three, six or nine months of registration a more informative indication can be obtained of the quality of the output. Moreover, since not all linkages are successful, it is also helpful to record the number of children who fail to remain with the foster/adopted parent and are re-registered; the number of such disruptions provides further evidence of the quality of the service. In measuring performance it is sometimes useful to measure not only the positive outputs but also the negative aspects of performance, such as exam failure rates in an educational context, since this is one indicator of the quality of delivery.

Outputs should represent some delivery, service or result of special interest. It might be simply the number of clients seen, or the number of client diagnostic profiles completed without error, or number of clients very pleased with the service. As in the case of inputs, outputs must be quantifiable and measurable. It is also common to define outputs in a qualitative way, such as 'completed without error' or classified as 'very pleased' – in other words, outputs must be in accordance with agreed quality specifications. Deciding which outputs are to be used in assessing efficiency and effectiveness is crucial to the performance measurement process.

Where outputs are not evidenced by events which can be counted, then other means of quantifying output must be devised. A charity formed to make authorities more aware of problems of drug dependency may use indirect measurement of outputs by counting the usage of its library or the pages of information issued, but it may also need to carry out surveys from time to time in order to assess the quality of its output. But here it is useful to distinguish between outputs and outcomes.

Outcomes

We cannot always quantify outcomes in the short term or with precision, nor do we need to try for operational performance measurement purposes, since outcomes are by definition somewhat remote from operational activity. Operational activity is managed on the expectation that desirable outcomes will follow from the planned outputs. Thus a charity formed to protect endangered gorillas in Rwanda may properly consider outputs to be the number of ranger hours spent in patrolling the chosen area, or the number of poachers apprehended, or the number of traps destroyed, all outputs which can be recorded and inter-preted and all of which may be assumed to contribute to the desired outcome even if that outcome cannot itself be precisely quantified except infrequently.

Outcomes are at a higher, more strategic, level than outputs. They need to be reviewed, together with the assumptions which link outputs to outcomes, on a regular but long-term basis as part of the strategic monitoring of performance. The fact that outcomes are remote and that it is often difficult to establish a cause and effect relationship between operations and outcomes is no reason for failing to assess the outputs at the operational level. Indeed, it is only by measuring outputs that we can complete the task of mea-suring charities' performance. Some religious charities may be seeking outcomes which cannot be scientifically measured but they should do so by means of outputs which can be measured, perhaps in terms of parishioner visits, church members recruited, attendance at services or even cash offerings collected.

At an even higher level, the assumption that relief of poverty and the advancement of education are a good thing and deserv-ing of support under charity law are rarely questioned since they have been considered self-evident for several generations. The interface between charities and the welfare state is none the less a movable boundary, aspects of which politicians consider in most government terms of office.

The main point to make about collecting data on both inputs and outputs is that the data should provide information appro-priate to the objectives of the activities of the charity. As was observed previously, information on one aspect of performance alone is of little help. Absolute figures rarely help in assessing performance. It is only when figures are used together as ratios or are compared with previous figures, or with figures from com-parable organisations, that useful conclusions can be drawn.

Key ratios

As we saw in Chapter 3, the relationship between objectives and inputs helps to assess economy, the relationship between inputs

and outputs helps to assess efficiency, while the relationship between outputs and objectives allows effectiveness to be
evaluated.

The concept of using a few key ratios to measure performance
is common in the profit sector, where there are many management guides on the subject, (for example, Westwick 1973) and the
financial press is continually reviewing ratios such as dividend
yields and price/earnings ratios. We are accustomed to monitoring performance whenever we drive a car, and we look mainly at
two ratios – miles per hour to gauge the speed, and the proportion of the petrol tank which is full to ensure we do not run out of
fuel. Some management writers (see Meyer 1994) have suggested
that management information be presented in the form of a
dashboard with the key performance measures displayed as
dials, of which there should be no more than 15, in order to
maintain attention to the key measures.

Charities do not seem to be very good at monitoring their
performance in this way. Research carried out in 1994 in a sample, some 50 charities found that only 17% of small charities and
44% of large charities commonly considered any financial ratios
when looking at their financial results. A higher proportion, 50%
of small charities and 75% of large charities, commonly considered non-financial indicators at formal meetings, but in most
cases these were simple volume or number counts and rarely
ratios indicating efficiency of effectiveness (Wise 1994).

It is perhaps more difficult to generalise about which ratios
should be used in charities than it is for businesses because of the
lack of a profit motive. The managers and trustees of charities
therefore have to give more thought to what are their key result
areas and which ratios can be used best to indicate performance.
Some examples, using not-for-profit organisations in the public
and voluntary sectors, are considered below, together with some
procedures which may be used for improvement.

Economy

Economy, that is the concept of paying no more than necessary for
the resources needed, is probably of least concern in charities. We
do not often, with some notable exceptions, think of charities as

being flush with money, so charities tend to be rather mean about spending. Much of their labour is provided by volunteers and even when paid staff are employed it is likely that salary levels will be somewhat behind those in the commercial and business sectors, perhaps tied to Civil Service grades of some sort.

This in itself does not guarantee economy, of course. The Audit Commission (1995), in a study of over 300 local authorities, found vast variations in salary levels for jobs of similar responsibility, with some officers in the same authority being paid twice as much as others of equal rank, and it was reported that some chief executives in shire districts earn six-figure salaries – higher than those paid in any London borough. These comparisons suggest that there is a lack of economy at a high level in some local government authorities.

A sign in a jewellers shop once said 'If you pay too much you may lose some money; if you pay too little you may lose everything' – a reminder that economy is not about paying as little as possible but about paying the right amount having regard to the need. Buying the cheapest computer system has often proved to be an expensive mistake made by some small – and not so small – charities, for example.

Nevertheless, the absence of the discipline of a bottom-line profit means that trustees must always be vigilant about economy. The financial regulations of the charity should ensure that any substantial purchase is subject to tender and that officers do not simply take the first offer or deal automatically with their favourite contacts.

One way of keeping an eye on economy is to review percentage running costs regularly both to establish the main costs to which attention should be directed and to pick up any adverse trends which might suggest the emergence of diseconomies. This performance measure is commonly used, for example, in executive agencies such as the Intervention Board, NHS Estates, the Occupational Health Service and others (CIMA, 1994).

It is also necessary to guard against waste of resources. Trustees would want to see that regulations are in place, and in use, to check that goods and cash received are properly recorded, subject to internal control procedures, and that stock control and stocktaking systems are applied where relevant. If significant, performance measures may be designed specially to monitor waste – for example, the Social Security Benefits Agency targets specified savings through the prevention and detection of fraud.

Value management – which includes value engineering, to identify or design requirements in advance; and value analysis, to improve existing service specifications – seeks to optimise value by discovering and avoiding unnecessary cost or waste. The value of resources may be expressed as the function they serve divided by their cost, recognising that value is increased either by improving the functions relative to cost or by reducing costs relative to function.

Efficiency

The relationship between inputs and outputs, often called productivity, is of special importance in a profit-seeking environment but is also important in a not-for-profit context. The quotation (NCVO 1981) at the beginning of this chapter may be a proper response in a philanthropic sense but it shows no regard for efficiency.

A more helpful view is encapsulated in the foreword to CIMA (1992) which starts:

To most people the concept of making a profit or having a 'surplus' arising from sick people is distasteful. Yet almost everyone accepts that the only way to provide better treatment for patients out of finite sums available is to improve the use of those resources. The problem is how to combine caring for health and life, which are beyond price, with the practical fact that if the cost per effectively treated patient is reduced, more patients can be treated.

It goes on to say 'How much is allocated to national health care and who pays for it and how – is political and a matter for politicians'; but 'How the funds provided are used to give best healthcare for all who need it – is a matter of good management'. Efficiency is about getting the greatest benefit from limited resources or conversely expending the least resources to obtain a given benefit.

In a business context it is normal to compare the cost of a product with its sales price as an indicator of efficiency. This may not be possible in a charity which does not sell its services at a market price. Proxy values may be used, however; thus a charity which finds foster homes for children in care may properly claim that the value of the service is at least the cost of keeping the child in care. Similarly, a charity seeking to prevent ex-prisoners from reoffending could value its successes by reference to the cost of keeping a prisoner in jail.

Even without a market price the cost per unit is a ratio which should be monitored. This is one of the most basic business calculations, yet it is surprising that many charities have no idea of the cost of the unit of service which they provide. Without it, it is doubtful if managers can form a judgement about value for money, monitor their efficiency, or make informed decisions about the best use of their resources. The Vehicle Certification Agency and the Forensic Science Service are examples of executive agencies which are targeted to achieve specified unit costs as performance measures.

The use of resources need not be measured in value terms, of course, in order to devise performance indicators. Where labour is a principal resource, as is common in many charity services, then time spent may be a good measure of inputs. Thus, the Passport Office monitors the time taken to handle applications as a performance measure.

Return on capital employed is not often appropriate in not-for-profit organisations but, where capital is important, as in much of the NHS, then ratios relating output to capital employed – ratios showing capital utilisation – should be monitored. The Royal Mint, for example, an agency which requires substantial capital employed in its operation, is expected to earn a percentage return on its assets.

Where several services are provided by a charity, especially when the services are intangible or qualitative, it is by no means easy to allocate common costs to particular services or to decide on what constitutes a unit of output for costing purposes. Here it is important to choose outputs and not outcomes. It would make little sense for the RNLI to calculate its costs per life saved, since it is doubtful if such information would be useful (though if the NHS were responsible for the life-boat service, it might take such a ratio into account in prioritising its allocation of funds between competing lifesaving opportunities). The cost per life-boat station and the utilisation of life-boats would be relevant performance indicators perhaps. The saving of lives is the strategic purpose of RNLI and lives saved is an outcome for strategic review, but it is too remote from operational efficiency, where life-boat services in readiness for emergencies might be considered more appropriate operational outputs.

The conversion of input resources into output service benefits may not be a simple one, and to address efficiency it is necessary to consider the various processes which are involved. Implementation of improvements in efficiency may be made on a step by step incremental basis or sometimes a major reorganisation of processes may be required, and the term *business process re-engineering* has recently become a fashionable way of describing this action.

The Victoria and Albert Museum's *Corporate Plan 1994–98* is built round a conceptual framework of inputs–processes–outputs. The plan recognises four main inputs: people, information technology, safety and security, and support services. There are four main forms of output: museum displays, exhibitions, publications and education. Similarly, the planning document identifies four main processes by which resources are used to generate outputs: collections management, building management, research activity and the museum knowledge base.

Very often there is a limit to the amount of output which can be achieved. In such cases an important measure of efficiency is the ratio of output to the limiting resource factor. This is frequently seen as a percentage of capacity utilisation. For example, the V&A, in common with most museums and art galleries, seeks to attract as many visitors as possible to its collections. It is clearly important, therefore, to record and monitor the number of visitors. At the same time there is a limit to the number of visitors who can comfortably and safely use the building and its facilities. Expressing actual usage as a percentage of estimated full capacity usage helps in assessing performance. By analysing capacity utilisation by time period and by gallery, policies (differential pricing, extended opening times, more targeted resources, perhaps) may be devised to improve the use of resources as close to full capacity as possible.

Effectiveness

Probably the most important performance measures in charities are those showing how successful the charity is in achieving its objectives. After all, there is little point in being very efficient if results are unsatisfactory. Effectiveness tells us whether we are *doing the right thing;* compare this with efficiency, which is *doing the thing right*. The quotation at the start of this chapter suggests that begging is a most efficient form of charity – but it is unlikely to be a very effective form of charity.

Measures of effectiveness require a comparison between outputs and objectives. This is often more difficult to measure than efficiency since the quality of outputs, as well as the quantity, are likely to be of prime importance. Where objectives are related to research or to public understanding of a problem or to client well-being, for example, it can be difficult to measure output directly. In such cases indirect measures of performance must be devised using key output measures which indicate progress towards the desired outcomes. Project milestones may be appropriate in a research environment – completion of tasks to time and cost targets or client satisfaction surveys.

Historic royal palaces are set performance targets based on improvements in visitor value-for-money rating and the Recruitment and Assessment Services Agency has a target percentage overall customer satisfaction rating; the Driving Standards Agency has a performance target of the percentage of telephone calls answered within one minute; the Central Veterinary Laboratory aims to achieve 80% of its research and development milestones; while HMSO aims to have 100% of orders delivered without fault (CIMA, 1994).

Quality

Fitzgerald *et al.* (1991) suggest a framework for assessing the quality of performance, depending, first, on whether the information is based on internal control data or on external customer feedback, and second, on the time the data is obtained – before, during or after delivery (Table 5.1).

The old-fashioned concept of production quality control relied on internal inspection, but modern total quality management practices try to build in control as early as possible, when poor performance can be avoided rather than corrected, and to involve the client as much as practicable, to ensure maximum satisfaction.

Table 5.1 A framework for quality assessment

	Pre-delivery	During	Post-delivery
External client satisfaction measures	client involved with specification specification negotiation	client assessment during process service sampling	client views after event after-sale survey
Internal quality measures	quality management specifications value management systems	quality control samples management inspections	quality audit report monitoring procedures

Source: Fitzgerald *et al.* (1991)

Charities are designed for beneficiaries and it goes without saying that measures of effectiveness should take the interests of the beneficiaries into account wherever possible. In charities dealing with disability, it is sometimes the case that clients with disability feel a lack of empathy with professional managers who may know about the disability academically but are perceived as not understanding it emotionally. Trustees should try to see that such beneficiaries are represented in the specification and delivery of services as well as, of course, in the monitoring of results after delivery. When the degree of disability is severe or where the beneficiaries of the charity are unable to communicate or contribute to the setting of standards, then their power is negligible compared to that of other stakeholders. In such cases trustees need to be particularly thoughtful about how best to measure client benefit and the effectiveness of the service.

Interestingly, Gutch (1992) found that experience in the USA suggests that increased involvement in contracting is likely to increase the powers of the paid staff, and one of his recommendations was 'that voluntary organisations should give priority to ensuring appropriate ways of involving users in planning, managing and monitoring service provision'.

In deciding what measures of effectiveness to monitor it is important to decide what measures of service will be treated as outputs for regular operational control and what will be regarded as outcomes for less frequent strategic review. A charity, formed to help clients with mental health problems by finding them work, measures its output in the number of clients undertaking rehabilitation work each week. A main measure of operational effectiveness is the proportion of available clients for whom work is provided – a weekly measure which is considered, and the trend monitored, monthly. The desired outcome, however, is that clients should be rehabilitated and become independent and able to seek their own employment opportunities. For strategic review of effectiveness, therefore, appropriate performance measures might be the proportion of clients who are discharged as being satisfactorily rehabilitated and the proportion who are able to obtain independent employment within, say, a year of their discharge.

So far we have considered effectiveness mostly in terms of non-financial measures, since these are probably the most relevant to a charity's mission. Non-financial measures should be considered in conjunction with financial ones, however, and the principal tool for doing so is through the budgetary control process. Budgeting is the usual way in which plans and objectives are quantified for approval. The process of comparing actual results with the relevant budget is in itself an important part of any performance measurement system and is the subject of the next chapter.

Conclusions and key points

Having agreed objectives, systems should be reviewed to make sure that the charity can capture information on inputs and outputs. It is the relationship between inputs, outputs and objectives which allows proper judgements about performance to be made.

Inputs are commonly recorded in value terms and, indeed, charities are bound to keep proper records to show what they have spent their money on. Inputs should also be recorded in non-financial terms, such as volunteer days or hostel bed/days, where the inputs are significant to operations, especially if the input supply is a limiting factor in the operations of the charity. Finance is itself frequently a limiting factor and for that reason performance indicators are certain to include cost ratios.

Performance measurement presupposes a good costing system, and this requirement has been underlined recently by the move towards contracting, whereby public services are deliverable by charities in return for payments based on the service level agreed and delivered instead of, as was more usually the case, on a general grant.

Charities should take advice on costing systems if necessary and, when negotiating contract prices, need to understand the effects of volume changes on costs and the fact that prices must reflect an appropriate element of overhead.

Charities' outputs are more likely to be expressed in non-financial measures. These may not be automatically produced by the charities' accounting systems and special procedures may have to be introduced to collect the statistics.

Outputs express the product of the activities which should in turn promote desired outcomes. Outputs by definition should be capable of quantification, whereas outcomes may be less precisely measurable and more remote from the direct influence of the charitable activities. Measuring outputs is essential to the process of assessing operational performance, whereas measuring outcomes can be less frequently undertaken as part of a strategic review process.

From consideration of objectives, inputs and outputs it is necessary to design measures of performance relevant to the organisation and to each manager whose performance is to be monitored. It is not possible to suggest a common set of indicators for charities in the same way as a general pyramid of ratios for a business can be postulated, but the aim should be to select a small range of measures, probably more than five but not more than ten for any manager, in the form of ratios covering economy, efficiency and effectiveness.

Procedures should encourage economy by requiring any major item of expenditure to be subject to tender; products or services should be designed to avoid unnecessary cost, that is any cost which does not ultimately add benefit by means of value analysis; and accounting or administrative systems should militate against fraud and waste.

The measure of operational efficiency will normally be expressed in terms of the key outputs per unit of key input. At the higher level, a suitable indicator of efficiency is the amount of money spent on charitable causes as a proportion of the total money collected. But this indicator, like any other, should not be used in isolation, and at lower levels it is often better to use physical rather than financial measures.

Measuring effectiveness is of the greatest difficulty in a charity because a charity's aims are more important than mere economic or financial aims so that neither objectives nor outputs may be financially quantifiable. Where it is possible to use proxy measures, such as opportunity costs, to assess the value of outputs, this should be done. Usually, however, it is important for a charity's trustees to devise ways of measuring outputs in non-financial terms which can be compared with the objectives which they have established for the charity.

6 Budgeting for performance measurement

> Budgeting is telling your money where to go instead of wondering where it went.
>
> (Anon)

Introduction

This book does not set out to deal with budgeting, especially since the subject is well covered in an earlier book in this series (Manley 1994), but budgeting is too important a part of the planning and control process to be entirely left out of a book on performance measurement. Budgets are the end-product of the planning process whereby the plans for the next year are quantified and authorised; and they are also the start of the control process whereby managers accept measurable objectives against which their actual results are compared.

The budget, by setting out agreed objectives, at least in financial terms, is an important mechanism in assessing effectiveness. Nearly all charities seem to be accustomed to using budgets. A survey in 1994 showed that virtually all large and medium-sized charities have regard to comparable budgeted income and expenditure figures when considering interim financial results. Even in the case of small charities with no more than 12 staff, 77% consider budget comparisons usually or always and a further 14% do so occasionally.

It seems that most established charities have taken note of the NCVO (1990) recommendations that voluntary organisations should use:

- an annual budget, specifying targets for the year, both in terms of sources of funds, expenditure to be incurred by the organisation (inputs), and the charitable objectives to be achieved (outputs);

- production of regular management information during the course of the year, examining progress against the budget and identifying action points where progress is at variance with budget expectations.

In this chapter, therefore, it is intended to review how budgets may be used in establishing procedures for measuring and monitoring operational performance, in linking strategic and operational management, and in reconciling top-down and bottom-up management styles.

Traditional budget methods

Budgeting is, of course, an old-established management tool. In the public sector it is used restrictively to delimit and authorise expenditure and is part of the constitutional means whereby Parliament empowers government to raise money each year for agreed purposes. In the private sector it is viewed more constructively as a management tool, and became particularly important in the context of standard costing and budgetary control when there was a large expansion in mass production in the first half of this century.

Standard costing and budgetary control involves using both quantities and value in the budget process in such a way that variances between actual and budget expenditure can be explained as price variances or as efficiency variances. Thus the monthly labour cost in a jewellery manufacturer might be budgeted as (300 hours at £12 per hour =) £3,600. The actual cost of production might be (330 hours at £11.50 per hour =) £3,795, giving an adverse variance of £195. The standard costing variances show that this is made up of:

	£
Adverse efficiency variance (30 hours at £12)	−360
Favourable rate-of-pay variance (330 at 50p)	+165
Net adverse variance	−195

This analysis assists management to understand its costs and to take steps to improve cost control or pricing policy. Standard costing and budgetary control methods are particularly suited to the production of standard goods where the main costs are variable direct costs, typically mostly direct labour and materials.

During the second half of this century there has been a steady trend away from the preponderance of direct costs and towards indirect costs. Overall there has been a trend away from manufacturing towards service industries in the UK, and even in manufacturing there is less reliance than formerly on direct labour and more on automatic robotic and technical facilities, which tend to appear as overhead costs and depreciation charges; there has been a trend away from standard goods towards more consumer choice and tailored product specifications and there has been a rapid reduction in the time which can be taken in responding to changes in customer demands and to competitors. At the same time management styles have had to become less authoritarian and military and more democratic and delegated.

All these changes have made it ever more important to find ways of understanding overheads and controlling all those indirect costs whose benefits are so difficult to measure precisely and whose outcomes are often difficult to calculate – research and development, public relations, promotion, management and administration, and so on – hence the emergence of budget techniques designed to address this need. There is also a need for the budget to be seen not simply as a mechanism for top management to impose targets on operational managers, but also a means of involving and motivating those managers.

Charities, by their nature, tend to have a special interest in these developments; they are concerned with the provision of (often intangible or subjective) services and they often exist in an environment where the non-pecuniary motivation of staff and volunteers is vital to the proper delivery of the service.

Zero-base budget principles

A first step in reviewing budget procedures is to review the management structure itself. The cascade of objectives described in Chapter 4 implies an extended chain of management in a large organisation, whereby general top-level objectives are translated into more detailed sub-objectives at the operational level at which resources are used to provide inputs – and convert inputs into outputs – to meet objectives. The front-line operational managers, who are able to take decisions which commit resources, are the managers who should be involved in the budget process. These managers are also likely to include those who have closest contact with the beneficiaries of the charity, and therefore closest understanding of their needs.

The identification of budget managers should be confirmed by the review and, by considering the objectives of each manager and their role in the overall objectives of the organisation, the reporting structure should also be confirmed.

Performance measurement is a process which can be carried out at any level, for a charity, a sector or a country at one extreme; or for microscopic operations within a process at the other extreme. The confirmation of budget centres is a practical recognition of the way in which control is delegated within an organisation. It defines the structure of activities for which managers are responsible and which together make up the organisation as a whole.

As well as reviewing the management structure, budget practice should also be considered. It is common, when it is time for managers to prepare their budgets, for each manager to take as his starting-point either last year's budget or the latest estimates for the current year. This is a convenient procedure and one which is sometimes formalised by setting out last year's budget in the first column of a spreadsheet, adding a column for known additions or deletions, applying appropriate inflation factors to each line of expenditure and cross-adding the columns to arrive at the new budget. If one of the principal purposes of a budget is to enable an organisation to look ahead and to allocate resources in line with expected needs, then this procedure is not very effective; it simply tends to perpetuate a previous pattern of expenditure, whether or not that pattern is optimal.

It is preferable to adopt a zero-based approach, that is, one where there is no prior assumption as to funding. A manager is expected to justify his entire budget from scratch, not by reference to any historical trend but by reference to the objectives which he has agreed to meet.

Statement of purpose

The starting-point for each operational manager, therefore, is to set out what are perceived as the essential objectives for the unit and to agree that statement with his/her boss. By repeating this process up the organisation hierarchy to the highest levels we are confirming, or if appropriate modifying, the cascade of objectives which lead down from the corporate mission to the operating units. This process alone will clarify understanding of the organisation structure and what it is designed to achieve. It is a process which allows the governing body to check how its mission is communicated to, and carried out by, operational managers.

At this pre-budget preparation stage, it is also good practice for each manager to consider how the activities of the unit further the agreed objectives, whether alternative activities or methods might be more desirable, and whether any changes are indicated to structure or working practices. It might be appropriate, for example in the interests of economy, to consider whether activities should continue to be handled in-house or contracted to external sub-contractors.

At this stage each budget-centre manager can complete a statement-of-purpose document (see Figure 6.1) which identifies the budget centre by name and code, and contains:

- a statement of the core objectives of the budget centre;
- a record of the manager responsible for the centre, to whom the manager reports and any sub-budget-centre managers who report to this centre;
- a brief note on present methods employed, including any alternatives considered but ruled out for the time being; and
- a note on other budget centres whose activities need to be co-ordinated with this centre to achieve the objectives of the centre.

To this statement-of-purpose document will be attached in due course the budget option statements for that unit, as described below.

Activity-level options

After agreeing the purpose of the unit and its place in the structure, the budget-centre manager will prepare a budget in the

Dept/Budget centre _____   Code no._____
Objectives of this department:
Main activities carried out:
Alternatives considered:
This budget centre reports to _____ the following budget centres report to this budget centre _____   _____ _____   _____
Submitted by: _____   Date: _____

Figure 6.1 Specimen statement-of-purpose form

usual way. However, under priority-based budgeting procedures, the manager should prepare not one single budget but
rather three options. The first budget option should set out the
minimum resources required to fulfil the most basic objectives of
the unit. It should entail a lower level of expenditure than is
currently the case and may not represent as professional a service
as the manager would wish to provide. It is the lowest level of
service possible, in the sense that the manager would be able to
say that, if this level of funding were not agreed, then the unit

should be closed down, since it would not be worthwhile retaining it.

The first-level budget should be summarised on an activity statement form (see Figure 6.2) showing:

- budget-centre identification;
- level (for example, in this assumption level 1 of 3);
- description of activities at this level;
- schedule of budget resources required in detail, with number of staff and all costs in value;
- a statement of what outputs will be achieved in return for the resources and how they can be measured; and
- a statement of the consequences to the organisation if this level of resourcing were not to be agreed.

The activity statement is principally a financial budget schedule, but the last two items listed above are most important for prioritisation purposes. For performance measurement the section on outputs and the measurement of outputs is essential and, in this section, the quantification of outputs in non-financial terms, as well as financial terms if relevant, is required.

The same activity statement form should be used again to set out the additional resources (costs), and the additional outputs, over and above those already requested at level 1, in a second statement. This will have the same sections as before, except that this statement will represent level 2 of 3. This level would probably provide a similar level of service to that currently provided.

Finally, assuming that three steps were appropriate, the manager should submit a third statement, level 3 of 3, setting out what extra costs over those already included in levels 1 and 2 he / she would wish to incur in order to provide an enhanced level of service or benefit above that currently provided. Managers typically complain that they have insufficient resources to do all the things which they would like to do. This requirement for a higher level of budget request allows every manager the chance to be innovative. It insists that managers quantify what extra resources they would like and what additional benefits they would provide with such resources. It positively encourages new ideas and the possibility of change.

The description above assumes that a budget centre has three levels of service at which it could operate. In practice, managers

Dept/Budget centre _____	Code no._____			
Level _____ of _____	Rank _____			
Description of this activity and operational objectives	Resources required			
	Description	Staff FTE Costs		Other Costs
		No.	£	£

How achievement of objectives measured;
Outputs to be realised:

Consequences if this level is not approved:

Justification	This activity level is	This activity should be coordinated with other centres:
Legal Requirement ☐	Less than ☐	
Policy Requirement ☐	Equal to ☐	_____
Tangible benefit ☐	More than ☐	_____
Intangible benefit ☐	Current levels	_____

Figure 6.2 Specimen budget option form

may recognise a greater number of feasible steps from minimal level to an enhanced level, but three should be the minimum number allowed, unless the budget centre is new, in which case a minimum of two would be appropriate.

This completes the budget preparation stage, at which stage the statement of purpose and the three or more activity statements can be put together as a package for subsequent consideration through the process of ranking the options.

Ranking or prioritisation

After the unit managers have prepared their packages the next stage is the ranking process, whereby the various options are considered and weighed against each other in order to determine priorities. Assume, for example, that a senior manager has three subordinates, each of whom has prepared four options relating to his/her own section. The manager will have 12 separate forms requesting funds which must be ranked in order of importance. Conceptually, if each form is regarded as a card, then the senior manager might rank the options by placing what he regards as the most important card at the bottom of the pack and so on until, at the top of the pack, is placed the option considered least worthy of financing.

For example, with three departments – A, old-established and very important; B, old-established but not now important; and C, a proposed new service – the overall manager might rank as follows:

1	Highest priority	A 1 of 4
2		A 2 of 4
3		C 1 of 4
4		A 3 of 4
5		C 2 of 4
6		B 1 of 4
7		A 4 of 4
8		B 2 of 4
9		C 3 of 4
10		B 3 of 4
11		C 4 of 4
12	Lowest priority	B 4 of 4

At this stage there is no question of approving or not approving the requests for funds. All that happens is that the manager arranges all requests for funds in order of importance as he/she sees it in the light of objectives, first by agreeing subordinates' rankings and second by comparing the requests of different subordinates.

There is no need to value outputs in order to prioritise. In not-for-profit organisations it is often impossible to quantify in financial terms (say) the value of the benefit of hip-replacement operations compared with heart by-pass operations, nor is this necessary. The prioritising manager does not have to quantify the difference in priorities but simply has to exercise judgement in deciding the order of preference with regard to the costs and benefits in question.

The senior manager will then take the pack of 12 options to his/her own more senior manager, who will similarly be receiving other option packs from the other managers within the division, and will amalgamate the various options in order of priority as he/she sees it. This procedure is repeated up the organisation hierarchy until it reaches the governing body of the organisation, which will by this time have accumulated all ideas for spending money in the organisation, ranked by succeeding levels of management within the organisation in order of agreed priorities relative to the objectives of the organisation.

The priorities may be readily summarised on a priority ranking form showing in rank order from highest priority to lowest:

- budget-centre reference;
- activity reference and level;
- activity budget cost;
- number of staff for the activity;
- cumulative budget cost up to and including the activity;
- cumulative number of staff up to and including the activity.

At the very end of the priority listing the cumulative totals will show the total amount requested and total staff required to operate every single request from every budget manager. By going down the list to the point at which revenue expected to be available is equal to the cumulative expenditure budget, it is possible to determine the cut-off point above which budget requests are agreed and below which they are refused.

For example, using the limited priority listing given earlier for one division only, the ranking might appear as in Table 6.1. Assuming that the maximum expenditure for this division were to be limited to £600,000, then the budget options 1–6 above would be approved. Those numbered 7–12 would be refused – not because they are necessarily undesirable ideas but because

Table 6.1 A priority ranking table

			Option		Cumulative	
			Staff no	£'000	Staff no	£'000
1	Top priority	A 1 of 4	6	84	6	84
2		A 2 of 4	4	63	10	147
3		C 1 of 4	10	150	20	297
4		A 3 of 4	3	44	23	341
5		C 2 of 4	4	72	27	413
6		B 1 of 4	8	118	35	531
7		A 4 of 4	5	75	40	606
8		B 2 of 4	7	96	47	702
9		C 3 of 4	5	80	52	782
10		B 3 of 4	4	60	56	842
11		C 4 of 4	0	40	56	882
12	Least priority	B 4 of 4	3	55	59	937

there are limited resources and other ideas for spending which are considered to have higher priorities.

Where the budget centres and budget costs are properly coded, the new budget can be printed out immediately, if it is well organised, using a simple data-base program. This simple description sounds somewhat mechanistic and in reality will not be quite so easy. There will be much discussion concerning the availability of income, the level of reserves, the level of expenditure and the relative merits of options close to the cut-off line. It is likely that options close to the cut-off will need to be re-examined at some length, but this concentration of management attention on the margin at which resources become too scarce to meet all demands is a major benefit of the process.

Managers often express concerns about this approach. Four such concerns are briefly addressed here.

The first is that it is difficult to hypothesise about lower levels of service than currently provided. This is true and it is sometimes forced by asking budget managers to budget the lowest level as current expenditure less (say) 20%. It is a somewhat artificial process and for that reason it is essential that any zero-base budget programme should be totally supported by the top management team.

The second concern is that the method of ranking options is good at strengthening the vertical management chain but does not encourage horizontal coordination of activity. This concern should be addressed by appointing a senior management committee to steer the budget process.

Thirdly, there seems to be a danger that lower-level managers will take inconsistent decisions. This concern is a subset of the previous one. It is overcome by the steering committee setting guidelines on common assumptions on, for example, rates of inflation, salary increases, and the like.

Finally, the process seems to imply heavy paperwork and much management time. This is a fear which tends to be exaggerated, but in any case it is not necessary to undertake a full zero-base budget exercise each year. Ideally in a smaller charity it is recommended every three to five years in conjunction with the strategic review cycle. For larger charities it may be done in one division each year so as to cover the whole charity every three to five years on a rolling basis to coincide with the strategic planning cycle.

Benefits of better budgeting

The effort of looking so fundamentally at the budget process has a number of benefits, among them the following:

- Resources are allocated by reference to agreed objectives, not to past patterns of expenditure.
- Plans remain flexible until the last moment. Even after the budget is approved, if unexpected funds are received the next priority for funds will be readily identified; if there is an unexpected shortfall of income, the projects with least priority can be discontinued.
- Alternative courses of action will have been examined and new ideas generated.
- Funding decisions can be better presented both internally and to external funders; external funding requests can show the consequence of different funding level decisions.
- Decision-making processes, even in a large and complex charity, will involve better understanding of detail; no longer can the chief executive, for example, cut everything by 5%. He/she could cut the lowest-priority projects representing 5%

of expenditure, but this would mean giving up specific programmes and the consequences of doing so would be clear.

- Decisions on funding will have involved all budget managers in formulating requirements and the ranking will have been reached through a participative process encouraging commitment from all.
- Attention is concentrated on marginal areas where resource allocation is most critical.

Most importantly from the point of view of this book, however, the final overall budget will be supported by agreed statements and budgets for each manager, showing the objectives agreed for that section, the inputs required and authorised, and the quantified outputs which the manager has agreed to provide in return. This combination of objectives, inputs and outputs means that all the components exist for assessing value for money and for establishing performance measures relative to each manager.

Conclusions and key points

Budgets are traditionally thought of as financial management tools, but they are more than that. Budgets are an integral part of the planning and control systems and need to be used by all managers and adapted to serve the purposes of performance measurement.

Recent developments in budgeting make it particularly relevant to charities – the increasing inclusion in budgets of non-financial measures, the importance of specifying outputs and not just cost inputs, the emphasis on activity- and priority-based budget methods, and the use of budgets in controlling overhead expenditure.

Charities are accustomed to using budgets. It is a small step, therefore, to seek improvements in budgeting techniques as a way to improve performance measurement in charities.

Zero-base budgeting methods have important benefits for charities; they require managers to justify budgets on the basis of agreed objectives which are aligned to the overall mission for the charity; and they make no assumptions as to continued funding from year to year.

Zero-base budgeting methods are particularly supportive in a performance-measurement context because each manager must define unit objectives, specify inputs, consider processes and define quantifiable outputs. This provides all the ingredients for value-for-money review and for establishing performance measures relevant to each manager.

7 Competition and co-operation: too many charities?

A leading fundraiser has attacked the National Lottery as one of the least cost-efficient ways of raising money for good causes ever devised. Mr Drucker, a visiting professor at the London School of Economics, told the Royal Society of Arts that after prizes, taxes, costs and promoters' profits, just 25 per cent would go to good causes.

(Snoddy 1994)

Introduction

We considered earlier how the charity sector has no market mechanism which encourages less deserving charities to be taken over or wound up as might be the case in the commercial world. There is a danger that charities which have served their purpose will continue more or less indefinitely. The Charity Commission report for 1993 commented, 'In 1991 two ancient charities came to our notice', and went on to describe two charities which had been set up in favour of the freemen and freemen's widows using the proceeds from common land or Lammas rights in the Borough of Huntingdon. 'By 1990 the number of freemen entitled to benefit had diminished to 15 while the property of the charities, following the sale of some of the common land, had grown to such an extent that each freeman received £31,750 a year' (Charity Commissioners 1994, para. 105). The Commission applied to the Court and the class of beneficiaries was expanded so as to benefit the people of Huntingdon, including the relief of the poor, the promotion of education and the provision of recreational activities. Though this seems to have come to a satisfactory solution, one wonders how many other ancient charities exist which were set up to meet circumstances no longer relevant today.

Too many charities?

It is difficult for any newcomer to the charity field not to be struck by the large number of organisations all operating in the same or similar areas. For example, in the edition on my desk of *Charity Choice*, an encyclopaedia of charities to which organisations can subscribe as a means of putting their names in front of potential donors, there are 134 charities in the 'Family Welfare' section, which is one of the shorter sections. They range through the alphabet, including:

Association for Marriage Enrichment
Birth Control Trust
Christian Family Concern
Divorce Conciliation and Advisory Service
Exploring Parenthood
Family Welfare Association
Gingerbread
Home-start Consultancy
Institute of Marital Studies
Jewish Marriage Council
Kith and Kids
La Leche League
Maternity Alliance
National Family Trust
One plus One Marriage and Partnership Research
Parent Network
Relate
Single Parents Links and Special Holidays
Twins and Multiple Births Association
Voluntary Organisations Liaison Council for Under Fives
Working Mothers' Association
Young Women's Christian Association

I do not know all of these charities (though I am aware of similar ones not listed in the encyclopaedia), so I am not sure whether Parent Network provides services very different from those of Parentline, or Parent to Parent Information on Adoption Services, or the Parent Advice Centre, or Parents Anonymous, or Parents in Partnership, or Parents to Parents – to name some of the other family welfare charities listed under P. Probably they are all providing a good specialist service but this small extract of charity names demonstrates how difficult it must be, both for those needing help and those wishing to provide it, to identify appropriate organisations.

I came across an example of the fragmented nature of the sector when reviewing facilities for training workers with blind people for the Department of Health and Social Security a few years ago. One might assume that such a specific activity would be clearly defined and serviced, but a social services directorate report (Hill *et al.*, 1988) at the time noted that 'a large number of national voluntary organisations exist to provide services to the blind: Royal National Institute for the Blind, Partially Sighted Society, Guide Dogs for the Blind Association, Talking Book Service, National Library for the Blind, Student Tape Library, St Dunstan's and National Wireless for the Blind to name a few'. It recorded that 'services at local levels are provided both separately and jointly by statutory and voluntary organisations and that the degree of collaboration varies widely and sometimes there is none at all'.

In fact the main training of workers with blind people was carried out not by one of the national charities mentioned but by two regional charities, the Northern Regional Association for the Blind and the Southern Regional Association for the Blind, both of which were then financed in the main by core funding government grants. These two associations had long resisted attempts to get together to form a national association, notwithstanding a Royal Commission recommendation as long ago as 1889 that 'there should be greater solidarity among the institutions and an interchange of information between them, so that they should work harmoniously together'. The government divided grants for the purpose of training workers with blind people between the two associations and tried as best it could to encourage cooperation with the Royal National Institute for the Blind and to encourage support from the resources of the Guide Dogs for the Blind.

The sector is, of course, aware that it could be stronger and more coherent, and the NCVO (1990) working party on effectiveness felt it had particular responsibility for improvement by ensuring that support is widely available for

- setting and raising standards;
- promoting cooperation;

* reducing overlap;
* encouraging mergers where necessary;
* strengthening partnerships with funders.

Economies of scale

Each charity mentioned at the beginning of this chapter must keep records of its financial transactions, appoint trustees and probably an honorary treasurer and an auditor. They are all likely to need office accommodation, they must all comply with any legal requirements, and they all prepare entries for *Charity Choice* and engage in other fund-raising activity. This all seems to add up to an uneconomic structure for marshalling resources in aid of those in need. Who can doubt that, in the commercial world, many of the less efficient charities would have been taken over and that the limited number of products provided would have been provided by a smaller number of larger business brand managers?

One would expect that there must be economies of scale in charitable bodies which would favour the growth or amalgamation of smaller charities. Charities exist to convert funds from donors into benefits for those entitled to gain from the charitable purposes of the trust. Efficiency in this sense of input/output measurement can be indicated from the accounts of charities.

The resources coming into the charity are readily identifiable from the accounts, though the amount of expenditure regarded as benefiting the beneficiaries is less easily defined. The *Henderson Top 2000 Charities 1994* guide summarises income and expenditure. Expenditure by way of grants to beneficiaries is clearly of direct benefit to them. In addition, the Henderson data on operating costs (which are not fully published in the guide) include data on expenditure on service provision and on administration. Though definitions here are likely to be rather subjective, it may be postulated that expenditure on service provision gives a benefit to the beneficiary whereas administration costs do not – indeed, excessive administration costs will reduce the amount available for the purposes of the charity.

From a marketing or needs-identification point of view, small local operations are likely to be most desirable. But the proliferation of charities is likely to be wasteful of resources since it may be expected that administrative costs will be proportionately less in larger charities which can benefit from economies of scale.

To test this expectation a sample was taken from *The Henderson Top 2000 Charities 1994* covering the 25 largest, the 25 smallest, and 25 half-way through the list. The results are shown in Table 7.1, which compares the largest 25 charities in the data base with a median sample of 25 and with the smallest 25 charities in the data base.

The larger charities appear to be more efficient. Benefits to beneficiaries, measured by the sum of grants paid plus costs of service provision, accounted for 84% of the income of large charities but 68% in the case of the median sample and only 61% for the small charities. Administration costs, on the other hand, account for under 9% of large charities' income, 14% of medium-sized charities' and over 23% of the small charities' income.

There are large differences between charities, which makes further research desirable. The figures themselves are open to further analysis and updating and, of course, the value of services to beneficiaries is greatly understated because the accounts do not include the value of volunteer labour inputs and outputs. But the analysis so far undertaken does suggest that it would be in the interests of beneficiaries that smaller charities should be seeking mergers or alliances or at least finding ways to combine and share administrative functions.

Administration is not undesirable, of course, and a charity can suffer from too little administrative cost as well as from too much, so that we should be seeking to optimise the conversion rate of income into direct charitable expenditure rather than to maximise it (that is to say, we must strike a balance between efficiency and effectiveness).

However, it is clear that very low rates of conversion are not acceptable. The report of the Charity Commissioners for 1993 instances a case where a fund-raiser organising sponsored balloon races was found to be applying for charitable purposes little more than 3% of the total funds raised. The Commission used its powers to remove the funds and transfer them to another charity with similar purposes (Charity Commissioners 1994, para. 65). The Commission also refers to investigations carried out jointly

Table 7.1 Large, medium-sized and small charities in The Henderson Top 2000 Charities 1994

No of charities	25 Large		25 Medium		25 Small		75 Total	
Value of sample	£m	%	£m	%	£m	%	£m	%
Total income	2,524	100.0	34.9	100.0	13.16	100.0	2,572	100.0
of which public grants, fees, etc.	901	35.7	8.8	25.1	1.15	8.7	911	35.4
Expenditure								
Grants made	954	37.8	5.1	14.6	4.55	34.6	964	37.5
Service provision	1,284	50.9	18.6	53.3	3.41	25.9	1,306	50.8
Sub-total	2,238	88.7	23.7	67.9	7.96	60.4	2,269	88.2
Publications	26	1.0	0.4	1.1	0.13	1.0	27	1.0
Administration	268	10.6	5.0	14.5	3.06	23.2	276	10.7
Publicity and fund-raising	71	2.8	0.2	0.6	0.59	4.5	72	2.8
Other and exceptional	−131	−5.2	2.1	6.0	−0.07	−0.5	−129	−5.0
Total expenditure	2,472	97.9	31.4	90.1	11.67	88.7	2,515	97.8
Mean percentages								
Total income		100.0		100.0		100.0		100.0
of which public grants, fees, etc.		38.1		25.1		8.8		24.0
Expenditure								
Grants made		32.0		14.6		34.6		27.1
Service provision		52.3		53.4		25.9		43.9
Sub-total		84.4		68.0		60.5		71.0
Publications		1.6		1.1		1.0		1.2
Administration		8.7		14.4		23.2		15.5
Publicity and fund-raising		4.2		0.6		4.5		3.1
Other and exceptional		−0.6		6.0		−0.5		1.6
Total expenditure		98.3		90.1		88.7		92.4

with Merseyside Fraud Squad into the Leukaemia and Cancer Society Fund whose promoters were sent to prison, and comments that 'over £300,000 had been collected over a three year period, but only £8,500 had been used for charitable purposes. The rest had been swallowed up in expenses' (Charity Commissioners 1994, para. 68). Tom Lloyd (1993) instances the case of a professional telesales firm used to promote a ball in aid of a children's hospital appeal, and comments that 'revenue amounted to almost £80,000, but the hospital, whose urgent need for a capital injection to prevent closure had inspired the generosity of advertisers, received only 17 per cent of it'.

The ratio of expenditure on charitable objects to total income available is therefore an indicator of efficiency which trustees and managers should pay attention to. Evidence suggests that the ratio is better in larger charities and that smaller charities should be alert to opportunities of joint ventures, mergers or cost-sharing activities as means of improving efficiency.

A similar point emerged from the study designed to learn from the US experience of contracting referred to earlier (Gutch 1992) which recommended that 'larger voluntary organisations should assist smaller groups working in their field or locality through providing them with technical assistance, helping them develop coalitions with other small groups or forming partnerships with them'.

The small survey carried out recently into management accounting practices (Wise, 1994) suggests that charities are aware of the need to cooperate with each other. A high proportion of all charities in the sample (73%), and an even higher proportion of the larger charities (88%), reported that they had agreed arrangements for cooperating with another charity or charities. Most respondents reported that the main purpose of such arrangements was to share information or improve the quality of service, though a desire to reduce costs or to improve fund-raising was also relevant.

Benchmarking

Once performance measures are established they can be used for control purposes by providing comparisons. Actual performance can be compared with standards for the activity (though in general there are few such standards in the charity sector), with predetermined targets or budgets (derived from the budget process described earlier), over time (by looking at trends), or by comparison with similar activities elsewhere, either internally or externally.

An advantage of having so large a population of charities is that there should be ample scope for comparisons of performance and for recognising best practices from which all could benefit. One reason why the Audit Commission can carry out so successfully its mission to improve the value of services provided by local authorities is that it has several hundred more or less similar organisations to review. It is able in these circumstances to draw up league tables and to identify examples of good practice for organisations to emulate and of bad practice requiring further attention and corrective action.

As yet there is little evidence that charities are making much use of benchmarking as a means to assess their own performance and seek improvements. Although, as noted above, most charities cooperate with other charities, only 20% in the sample survey reported any arrangements for comparing their performance with that of another, and less than half of these could regard this as best practice benchmarking. There was much interest in the idea, however, since 57% of the sample and 75% of the larger charities reported that they would be interested in exploring opportunities for best-practice benchmarking. This alone would justify some further explanation of what is involved. Benchmarking has emerged recently as a recognised tool for comparing and assessing performance – and as a means of achieving continuous improvement programmes – and the remainder of this chapter looks at how benchmarking has developed and might be further used in assessing charity performance. The current interest in benchmarking has emphasised collaborative comparison of those processes which involve factors which are critical to the success of the organisation. Both performance measurement and benchmarking are therefore concerned with the same things. According to a Gallop survey of top UK companies conducted for the Confederation of British Industry, over three-quarters of top companies are using benchmarking targets to track their performance. The chairman of the CBI Manufacturing

Council is quoted as saying that 'Benchmarking can help us define our objectives more clearly, manage our resources and monitor our performance more objectively' (CBI Press Release, 1 July 1994).

As simply a form of comparative statistics, benchmarking has been used for years. The WM Charity Service, for example, was started in 1984 and now measures the investment returns on some 250 funds with assets of almost £6 million. In this sense industry averages may be used as a benchmark, but even in this financial area it is recognised that, because of specific constraints, individual charities may establish their own peculiar benchmark. For amplification of these comments and a full discussion of the assessment of investment performance, readers are referred to Harrison (1994).

Best-practice benchmarking as a recognised technique probably stems from its consideration by the US Department of Commerce's National Quality Award (NQA) board of examiners in 1989 and its inclusion as a key reason for the award in that year. In 1991 benchmarking was cited in 12 of the 32 NQA evaluation criteria. It is a part of the total quality management process, and benchmarking is not seen simply as a comparison against an industry average but as against the best in the class for the purpose of achieving and sustaining excellence. In view of its origins, much of the early material on benchmarking is from the USA, but more recently UK practices have received more attention and in 1993 a club, the Benchmark Network, was formed under the direction of the Quality Director of Royal Mail to encourage the practice of benchmarking and sharing of ideas and techniques for improving performance. The club caters for all sectors of business including the voluntary sector.

This illustrates the point that benchmarking can be carried out between different organisations; they do not need to be competitors or even within the same sector. Naturally, if a charity wished to benchmark its ability to attract legacy income, it would look within the charity sector for the organisation which appeared to manage this activity best. But other key processes might be handled best outside the charity sector, in which case non-charity businesses might be selected as best-practice benchmark partners. Xerox, an early promoter of benchmarking, is said to have selected American Express for invoicing, Florida Power for its quality management process and Cummins Engines for factory layout, for example. Benchmarking is focused on processes rather than on outcomes, and many processes are common to business and not-for-profit organisations alike. Commercial businesses already have many arrangements for sponsoring the voluntary sector. I hope that increasing opportunities will be found to encourage cross-sector benchmarking for the benefit of both parties.

It is essential for benchmarking that the partners should be willing to share information and undertake reciprocal visits, while respecting that there may be some sensitive information which will be kept confidential. The charity sector exhibits a lot of rivalry but is also made up of many cooperative and supportive organisations to which benchmarking should seem a natural way forward. A benchmarking partnership generally implies acceptance of a benchmarking code of good conduct, etiquette and ethics; the parties to such an agreement would be wise to record their understanding of the arrangements formally so as to avoid misunderstanding.

Benchmarking implies a willingness to change and a desire to excel. It may be a valuable tool for introducing change into a charity but it is a technique – like that of zero-base budgeting which we considered earlier – which can only be successfully introduced if it has the support of the governing body and its chief executive officer.

The phases in benchmarking have been classified as planning, data collection, analysis, implementation and recalibration.

Planning is both an organisation matter – who is to be responsible and with what team to report within what time-scale – and a deterministic matter. The latter requires first of all a decision on what processes to benchmark and what priorities to apply; a decision which will follow from consideration of the critical success factors stemming from the mission–means–measures process, which we looked at in Chapter 4.

After the target processes are identified it will be possible to identify the possible comparator organisations to be benchmarked. In seeking a partner, it is not the purpose to find the most successful partner but rather the one which is doing something especially well in the area to be benchmarked. No one organisation is likely to be best in every process. The selection of suitable partners means some research with clients or client group representatives, members of professional or trade associations, government or business directories, and management consultants or experts in the area.

Finally, the shortlist can be drawn up by verifying that the proposed partner is friendly and willing to share information and checking that the process to be compared is sufficiently close to produce valid results.

The most rewarding means of *data collection* is by way of direct contact and exchange of information, and this is likely to be most effective if preceded by some desk research to establish background knowledge in advance – the sort of material which can be obtained from annual reports, Companies House or Charity Commission returns, official publications or research reports, and so on.

Analysis of data collected tends to fall into two types: the measurement of performance in quantified terms, and the reasons why and methods by which it is achieved. The first measures are needed to assess the gap between your own performance and that of your benchmark partner. Understanding the reasons for the gap and their applicability to your own situation is the key to designing steps which will close the gap – or, better, will allow you to leapfrog it. The purpose of benchmarking is not simply to catch up with best practice in the chosen process but to gain a lead and to become best practitioner in the field.

Finally, benchmarking is a means to continuous improvement – a journey, not a destination. *Implementation* is not a final process, and the term *recalibration* is sometimes used to signify that best practices soon become out of date unless they are renewed. Understanding processes and how to improve them should lead to reiteration and further improvement. The Japanese quality car, the Lexus, used to refer in advertisements to features compared with other high quality competitors. In the national press I recently saw an advertisement showing an old model Lexus and the new model. It had the slogan 'We compared the Lexus to the best car in the world and it's better'.

Lessons from the public sector

Before leaving this chapter on competition and cooperation, it may be interesting to consider briefly how the public sector has responded to some of the difficulties facing not for profit organisations.

We have already referred to the way in which the government is requiring service units to prepare service level agreements which define and cost the service to be provided. Where services are provided through charities or voluntary sector organisations, the trend is for government to fund those services by way of contract payments per unit of service delivered in place of a previous grant in aid. This may raise a number of difficulties, some of which we have referred to previously, but it has the advantage of introducing quasi-market disciplines which in turn assist in the implementation of performance-measurement procedures.

In HM Treasury (1991) the government observed that in the past public service culture was more often concerned with procedure than performance and stated that The Government's programme of reform will continue into the 1990s with the aim of:

- making managers more accountable for performance within a clear framework of objectives and resources;
- distinguishing the roles of policy formulation and service delivery;
- introducing, wherever feasible, contracts and service level agreements which define standards of performance and responsibility for meeting them.

All these changes enable managers to focus on buying the best standard of service achievable within a given budget.

These measures are clearly designed to address issues of economy and efficiency.

The measures introduced by the government are also designed to improve quality in the sense of improved acceptability to the customer. The aim of total quality management is not simply to satisfy the customer but to delight him/her. Customers of public services, like the clients of charities, are generally in a weak negotiating position and are in danger of being treated in a patronising or offhand manner. The Citizen's Charter was introduced to instil good standards of customer service, and those standards may sometimes be a relevant example for a charitable body to adopt for its clients.

The Citizen's Charter set out six key principles which may be summarised as follows:

- The publication of standards of service that customers can expect and the comparison of actual performance against those standards.
- Consideration, in setting standards, of the views of those who use the service.
- Clear information about the range of services provided, in plain language.
- Courteous and efficient customer service from staff prepared to identify themselves by name.
- Well-signposted avenues for complaint if the customer is not satisfied, with means of independent review if possible.
- Independent evaluation of performance against standards and a clear commitment to value for money.

Customer focus is well established as a source of competitive advantage in the business world, and business managers have an interest in seeing that it is applied. In the public sector some motivation is provided by the award of the Charter Mark to organisations consistently delivering a high standard of service. For example, the Victoria and Albert Museum, to which we referred earlier, has won a Charter Mark. The museum asks those staff who work in back-office environments to do some weekend work in the galleries in order to gain a better understanding of the people for whom they are working – an arrangement likely to improve customer awareness and the effectiveness of the museum's work. Perhaps the Charity Commissioners might consider some similar award for those charities outside the public domain which demonstrate conspicuous excellence in serving their objects.

In a consultation paper, *Better Accounting for the Taxpayer's Money* (HM Treasury 1994), the Treasury attempts to tighten up on accounting for the effectiveness of public expenditure by suggesting that department financial statements of cost, cash flows and balance sheet should be accompanied two additional schedules – a main objects analysis (schedule D) setting out how much was to be spent, analysed by main objectives; and an output and performance analysis (schedule E) setting out, under each main objective recognised, the measure of performance used and the cost of the programme. This far-reaching proposal is still causing much discussion and dissension. However, if government departments are able to produce annual statements showing how their expenditure is devoted to main objectives and how they have costed and measured achievement of each main objective, it should be possible for charities to do likewise.

The Chartered Institute of Management Accountants action checklist for managers of public sector executive agencies (in CIMA, 1993) may be useful also to charity managers (if *beneficiary* is substituted for *customer*):

i)   don't wait for the performance culture to be forced on you but seize it as an opportunity. It can: focus your mind on what you are doing and why; drive you towards increasing efficiency and value for money; lead to greater customer satisfaction; and bring business opportunities;

ii)   be prepared to delegate responsibility before you delegate financial budgets;

iii)   train staff to understand what delegated responsibility means and provide them with the access to skills and opportunities for them to maximise their contribution;

iv)   set realistic performance targets that are driven by your business customers' needs as well as by the needs of central government or the Agency itself;

v)   constantly review performance and ensure that lessons identified are disseminated widely so that all can learn from them;

vi)   ask yourself whether you and your management colleagues are focusing on critical performance measures and whether you are spending enough time at management meetings appraising the implications;

vii)   communicate performance information simply and succinctly;

viii) encourage all staff to feed information up the management chain;

ix)   define for yourself who your business customers are, consult them and clearly identify their needs;

x)   continually monitor and improve the service your Agency provides. Monitoring should be both internal and external through customer involvement either through surveys or liaison groups. You should work towards involving customers in discussions on performance levels, both achieved and planned;

xi)   accept that you won't get everything right first time. You should be prepared to admit this but also be committed to helping your Agency continually improve its performance.

Conclusions and key points

Charities are easily formed but tend not to go under. Market forces which weed out unsuitable businesses do not apply with such force to the charity sector. It may be the case that there are too many charities operating and that the sector would benefit from some rationalisation.

This is borne out by some recent tentative research which indicates that the proportion of income used directly for charitable purposes is higher in large than in smaller charities; and conversely, that administration takes a lower proportion of total income in large charities than in smaller ones.

There is scope, therefore, for more mergers and cooperative and cost-sharing ventures in the charity sector.

Meanwhile, the existence of so many charities provides an opportunity for the assessment of performance using comparisons between charities to indicate good or less good practices. This should be taken further by greater acceptance by charities of the technique of best-practice benchmarking as a means of comparing operational performance with the best practices elsewhere in the sector or outside it. Benchmarking is a way of assessing performance in key process areas by reference to others who are the best practitioners in that field. It is a joint cooperative exercise which requires the friendly participation of both parties with a view to achieving continuous improvements in performance. The links with commerce and industry by way of sponsorships and donations could be further developed by benchmarking partnerships.

8 A strategic overview

> Strategic financial management . . . is relevant to all enterprises which have multiple stakeholders, because it is concerned with balancing the legitimate financial aspirations of such stakeholders.
>
> (Allen 1995)

Introduction

In this book on performance measurement we have covered a wide range of related subject-matter. After the early introductory chapters covering the background and theories relating to performance measurement, we concentrated on the need for vision in not-for-profit enterprises and on how this is translated into action through the mission of the organisation, critical success factors and the cascade of objectives down the management hierarchy – a top-down process considered in Chapter 4.

In Chapter 5 we examined more fully the inputs and outputs which need to be measured in order, by reference to the objectives of the organisation, to assess the three components of performance: economy, efficiency and effectiveness. We considered briefly the need to examine the processes whereby inputs are converted to outputs in devising ways to improve efficiency. We have stressed, when looking at effectiveness, the need for trustees constantly to bear in mind the interests of the beneficiaries, but we must also recognise the necessity of considering the donors whose money allows the charity to operate.

The interrelationship between these ideas is neatly illustrated in the *Corporate Plan 1994–98* document of the Victoria and Albert Museum, an exempt charity, which includes a diagram entitled 'A conceptual framework' consisting of six concentric rings

(Figure 8.1). At the centre is the mission of the V & A, and next to this is the audience, those people whom the V & A is seeking to benefit and influence. This, in turn, is surrounded by the outputs by which the audience is engaged; then the processes which produce the outputs; and beyond that the inputs into the various processes. The whole is surrounded by a circle representing the funding which is needed to finance the inputs.

In Chapters 6 and 7 we looked at two strategies for judging operational performance. Chapter 6 explored internal means of developing priorities and performance measures through budget mechanisms, particularly the bottom-up benefits of a zero-base

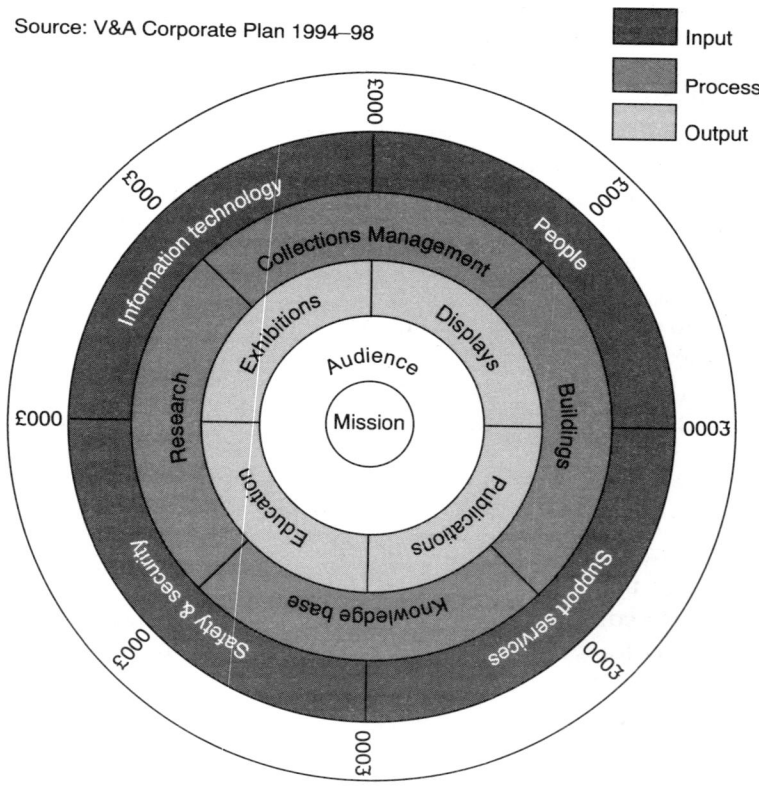

Figure 8.1 The Victoria and Albert Museum: a conceptual framework

budget approach. Chapter 7 outlined benchmarking as an external means of performance measurement and improvement.

Performance assessment cycles

In this chapter we return to some of our earlier thoughts. However, we do so from a strategic point of view with the intention of recalling some of the main areas into which trustees and managers need to direct their planning and control enquiries. We have already drawn a distinction between operational performance, which is essential for measuring and controlling the activity of the organisation, and strategic performance, which is necessarily a less precise but ultimately more important concept for long-term planning. The model showing the performance assessment steps in each cycle and how the two are connected was introduced in Chapter 4, but it is reproduced again here as Figure 8.2 to remind us of the ideas discussed earlier.

'Performance measurement' is a term generally applied to the operational cycle. In commercial organisations the operational cycle, which is quantified financially each year by the profit and

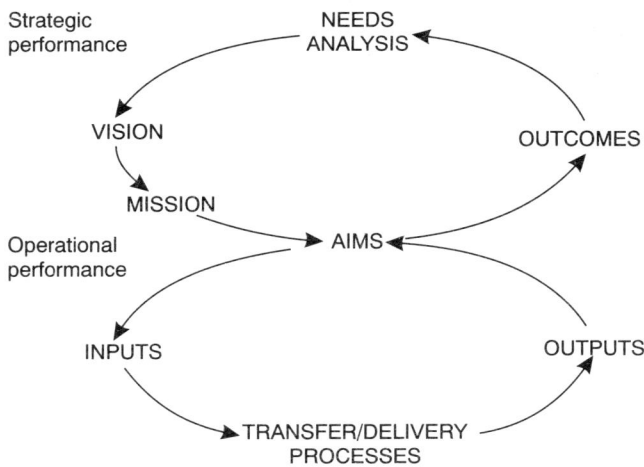

Figure 8.2 Figure-of-eight model for value for money (from Chapter 4)

loss account of the business, is treated as the major measure of performance. Businesses are sometimes criticised as being too short-term in outlook, but perhaps this is understandable if the main purpose of business is to make profit for the owners.

In charities, whose purposes are more important than financial gain, the operational cycle must be just as closely controlled as in businesses – not as an end in itself, but as a means to the end, the charitable mission for which the organisation was established. This requires the governing body of the charity to step back from the detail from time to time and to question the charity's ability to generate long-term value or relief for its beneficiaries.

Strategic review six-point model

The performance of the charity from this strategic point of view needs to be considered from several aspects, and I suggest that a strategic performance appraisal should encompass six points:

> *External focus:*
> How well are we satisfying defined needs of our beneficiaries?
> How well is our public image attracting support?
> How well are our relationships influencing government?
> *Internal focus:*
> How well do our resources and reserves match requirements?
> How effectively are volunteers and staff motivated?
> How well do we convert resources available into benefits?

By representing the internal and external aspects as triangles and laying one triangle over the other, the strategic review model can be represented as a six-point star, as shown in Figure 8.3. At the top of the star are the interests of the beneficiaries, since this is the object of the organisation. As has been emphasised many times before in this short book, the performance of the charity in relation to the intended beneficiaries is the primary consideration.

The beneficiaries' perspective

In reviewing the strategic performance of the charity from the beneficiaries' perspective it is appropriate to consider outcomes.

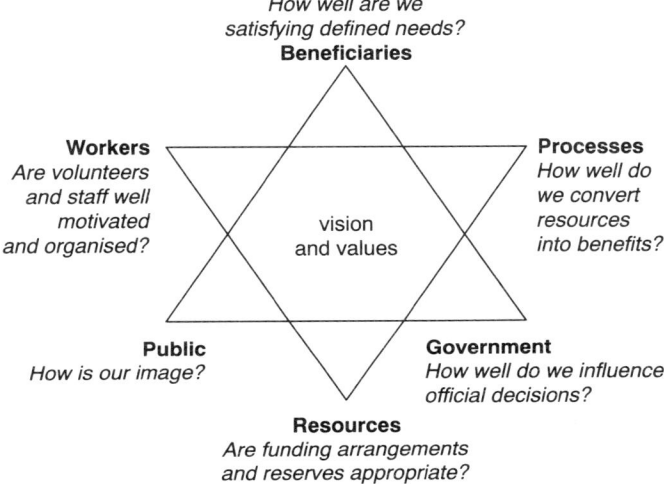

Figure 8.3 A six-point model for strategic review

In looking at operational performance, outcomes are too remote from processes or inputs to be used in calculating measures of efficiency and effectiveness; the working assumption is made that outputs will lead to desired outcomes. This assumption has to be questioned in the strategic review, and alternative means of attaining the desired ends should be considered.

The needs of the beneficiaries which are intended to be alleviated must also be questioned at the strategic review stage, since this is frequently an assumption based on historical circumstances which may have changed in the meantime. It is desirable to carry out a needs survey from time to time to ensure that needs are well understood and that the charity's aims properly address those needs. For example, the Social Services Inspectorate in a 1988 report for the government on the management and organisation of services for people who are blind or visually handicapped (Hill *et al.*, 1988), recommended, among other things, that:

- the needs of the visually handicapped population should be identified, and
- people with visual handicaps should be more involved in the running of voluntary organisations and to assist in the contacts with statutory agencies in order to strengthen relationships and credibility.

The first recommendation is obvious – but there had been no systematic survey of needs for many years before the report was written, so there was no clarity as to the appropriateness of service provision at the time. The second recommendation quoted above emphasises the importance, where possible, of involving beneficiary representatives in the strategic process to ensure that their perspective is appreciated and that they feel involved in the process. This is not always the case, although, at the time of writing, there has been favourable comment on the appointment of Doug Alker at the Royal National Institute for Deaf People as a sign of a fresh commitment to active representation of its client group.

Funders' perspectives

Just as a nation must create wealth before it can distribute it, so a charity must raise funds before it can apply them for its charitable purposes. The three points at the bottom of the six-point star model (Figure 8.3) are related to the organisation's ability to raise funds and illustrate that the stability of the charity rests on a fund-raising foundation. All three points need to be considered together since they are closely related, even though the importance of each one will vary from charity to charity. Some charities, particularly the foundations and endowment funds, have their own resources to generate investment income and can place the public and government relations points in a low strategic priority category. The Wellcome Trust, for example, generates enormous investment income with which to fund its medical research objectives and, while public relations and government relationships are not unimportant, there is no need for either public donations or government grants. For the sector as a whole some 17% of income is internally generated in the form of investment income or capital gains, according to research done for the CSO relating to 1990/91.

There are some charities – Guide Dogs for the Blind may be an example – whose appeal to the public is so strong that they can depend on a steady flow of income from the public without recourse to government support. Indeed, such charities are sometimes criticised for attracting funds surplus to requirements to hold as reserves. Income from private individuals is estimated to represent some 38% of total income for the sector; a further 10% is from companies; while another 8% is from grants from other charitable trusts. This aspect of strategic performance is of major importance, therefore, in the majority of charities.

Other charities – those designed to assist drug-abuse or AIDS victims for example – find it more difficult to attract support from the general public and must cultivate official central or local government backing for their services. The government has particular responsibilities in such cases, as the NCVO (1990) indicated when it observed in its conclusions on grant-giving: 'Government action to swell the overall pool of charitable donations is welcome, but it cannot be a substitute for grant-aid towards the core income of those voluntary organisations which do not have a popular appeal.' Over a quarter of the sector's total income is estimated to derive from government sources.

The relationship between the various sources of funds which a charity aims to attract is of strategic importance and is likely to influence the character of the whole organisation. The NCVO (1990), in commenting on the need for core funding, said: 'Without such core funding, enthusiasm, expertise and energy can be dissipated by having to maintain a vulnerable and incoherent mass of short-term funding sources in order to meet long-term commitments.'

Reserves policy

At this point it is appropriate to raise the question of reserves held by charities, since this is a subject which often receives unfavourable comment in the Press. In the corporate commercial sector reserves are undistributed profits. Any excess of income over costs may be paid to the owners as dividends or retained on their behalf as reserves in the business. The question of distribution policy is important for tax reasons and for implications on shareholder preference between income and capital growth. In a charity there is no question of distributing any surplus of income over expenditure to the owners; the question is sometimes raised more fundamentally as to whether there should be a surplus at all.

Reserves policy is a matter of balance. At one extreme, it is wrong for a charity to obtain money from donors which it fails to expend on charitable purposes. To obtain money for charitable purposes and retain it for no good reason seems to be a breach of trust and deprives current potential clients of benefits which they could receive. At the other extreme, it is neither practical nor sensible to synchronise the expenditure of funds exactly with income. If only for this reason, a charity may be expected to have some reserves. A very low level of reserves implies living from hand to mouth and, although many smaller charities have to do so, it is difficult to operate efficiently or effectively in circumstances where decisions can only be made within a short time-horizon.

Reserves are needed to balance present resources with future needs and are justified broadly on three counts. First, there is a short-term need for liquidity and working capital – reserves must allow for this as well as any seasonal peaks anticipated. Second, charities may have longer-term plans for development which require reserves to be accumulated in order to finance those developments. Third, some flexibility is needed to cover uncertainty – the risk that income will fall short of, or that expenditure will exceed, the expected figures during any planning period.

The former Director of Finance and Corporate Affairs at Barnardo's, which aims to maintain reserves equivalent to some 9–12 months' expenditure, suggests (Hind 1994) that each charity 'has to reach agreement on what is an acceptable operating range' for reserves for three reasons:

- it provides a basis for strategic planning
- it provides a defence against media and public criticism, and
- it improves the effectiveness of the decision making, overall, in the charity.

What is an appropriate level of reserves cannot be answered in the abstract but only by looking at requirements in each particular case and, naturally since the calculations are based on future forecasts, there is inevitably a degree of subjective judgement in determining the appropriate level. It is all the more important that a charity should have a reserves policy and should explain how it has established its reserves levels. This point has been endorsed by the NCVO (1990) working party on effectiveness in the sector when it recommended that charities should place more emphasis on explaining the purpose for which reserves are being held. Policies governing the retention of reserves, whether they represent cumulative surpluses on unrestricted funds or permanent endowment funds, should be clearly outlined. . . . In some instances, future commitments will justify, and indeed require, the retention of considerable sums. In other cases, large reserves might be due to the fact that the organisation has already received adequate funds and should now concentrate more on utilising existing funds effectively.

The relationship between the three fund-raising points identified by Hind (1994) was well illustrated by the director of a major grant-giving foundation which gave away grants in excess of £8 million in 1993. He gave the following examples of applications whose outcome was affected by reserve levels.

Example 1 related to a large, well-established charity with several reserves, designated 'building reserve', 'development reserve' and so on, as well as undesignated cash. The grant application to fund a new building was refused because the reserves were healthy and the applicants were unable to explain satisfactorily why they were unable to call on their own reserves.

Example 2 related to a charity which provided residential care for people with long-term and chronic illnesses and which had a high level (just over three years) of reserves. The foundation accepted the argument that high reserves were needed to guarantee to existing users, with a life expectancy of up to 15 years, that the charity could provide a lifetime of care, especially as it was uncertain that the various purchasers of accommodation would be prepared to maintain their financial commitments.

Example 3 was a medium-sized charity which sought a grant to strengthen its fee-earning potential and which had lowish reserves of about six months. The grant was turned down because the charity had a rock-solid donor base and legacy income which should have allowed the charity sufficient confidence to plan and arrange the work itself from its own income generation.

Example 4 was a lively and ambitious organisation which was three years old but had suffered from cash problems since its inception. The grant was turned down in this case because it was felt that the lack of any reserve position not only made it vulnerable but also suggested some lack of prudence and forward planning.

The director observed of committee members making applications for funds that:

It is crucial that they understand the accounts. Whilst the income/ expenditure pattern, the level of administration costs and the donor sources are likely to be well understood, questions concerning the balance sheet and reserves are less likely to be well handled.

(Carrington, 1994)

Public awareness

We have considered relationships with the general public and with government mainly from the perspective of fund-raising potential. It is often in a charity's interest, and part of its charitable purposes, to raise public awareness of an issue or problem with which it is concerned or to promote policies to the authorities.

These campaigning activities are not easy to measure on a day-to-day basis because they may take place over a long time and the results are not immediate and often uncertain. For these reasons the performance of campaigning activities needs to be undertaken regularly as part of the strategic review of outcomes and their relationship to the campaign outputs. The NCVO (1990) working party stated:

We believe that the trustees of each voluntary organisation . . . have a responsibility within the context of their objectives and powers, to review regularly whether the proportion of effort and resources devoted to campaigning, as opposed to services or other tasks, represents the most efficient mix of resources.

Process review

Between the fund-raising points discussed at some length above and the primary point of the beneficiaries' perspective are the other two points, whereby resources obtained are converted to benefits through the processes of the charity and the labour of its staff and volunteers. These points are likely to be under regular review as performance monitoring at the operational level considers the efficiency and effectiveness of the charity's processes on a regular basis. They are included in the model to ensure that both human resource policies and the processes themselves are given fundamental strategic consideration from time to time. Both areas are likely to be improved and modified incrementally as time goes by, but it is useful to start from scratch every three to five years and consider how well human resource policies are formulated, whether motivation is properly sustained, whether the mix of paid/volunteer staff is suitable and the interface well managed, and whether opportunities exist for cooperative ventures with other charities.

In the same way, the activities or processes should also be reviewed: are they still required, are they organised in the best way, should non-core activities be placed outside, can lessons or opportunities from outside be used? The fundamental review of processes to improve efficiency and add value to the delivery of services is currently a fashionable subject described by consultants as 'business process re-engineering'.

In reviewing activities, the following Rudyard Kipling poem is a good reminder of the steps required in a comprehensive review procedure:

I kept six honest working men
They taught me all I knew
Their names were What and Why and When
And How and Where and Who.

The six steps are summarized in Table 8.1.

Conclusions and key points

Performance measurement is often thought of as a short-term control mechanism, and, indeed, much of this book has been

Table 8.1 The six steps of a comprehensive review procedure

Existing process	Reasons	Alternative
What is the process?	Is it needed?	What else can be done?
Why is it done?	What does it achieve?	Are there better outputs?
When is it done?	Why then?	Can timing be improved?
How is it done?	Why like that?	Can methods be streamlined?
Where is it done?	Why there?	Could the location be improved?
Who does it?	Why them?	Can labour be improved?

concerned with measuring operational performance on a day-to-day, or at least on a month-to-month, basis. Alongside the operational performance measurement systems, however, trustees should also ensure that a strategic performance measurement system is in place.

The strategic performance measurement system does not require such frequent monitoring, nor can it be applied with such detailed and accurate measures, as the operational system. But the strategic review of performance is ultimately more important because it reaffirms (or not, as the case may be) the mission of the charity and the way in which the mission is implemented.

Strategic review of performance should involve a balanced view of stakeholder perspectives and activities within the charity. A model linking these includes three external perspectives (those of the beneficiaries; the public and those who provide funds directly; and the government which provides funds on the public's behalf) and three internal aspects of the charity's work (the charity workers themselves; the processes in the charity whereby value is provided to beneficiaries; and the reserves which exist within the charity).

Of the strategic review areas, the primary one is concerned with the perspective of the beneficiaries – those persons or objects for whom the charity was established and continues to exist. The review should redefine the extent of the need which the charity seeks to address, and it should review the objectives of the charity, that is, the means by which the needs are addressed. It will have been assumed that the means selected will lead to satisfactory outcomes which meet to some extent the needs identified. The strategic review should consider the appropriateness of outcomes relative to needs and the relevance of the chosen means to the outcomes.

The strategic review should cover the ability of the charity to attract funds, having regard to the charity's public image, its relationship with the government, and its own reserves.

A charity should establish a reserves policy as part of its strategic planning and performance-measurement policy.

Within the strategic review of performance, the charity should plan the relationship between trustees, paid staff and volunteer workers, as well as the way in which workers are motivated and rewarded and how their performance should be monitored. It should also examine the processes carried out to ensure that they remain appropriate and that they are carried out efficiently.

9 Some conclusions and recommendations

A time of change

There must inevitably be some diffidence in attempting to draw conclusions relating to a population as diverse as the charity sector. Moreover, circumstances are currently in a state of change. Some charities are affected directly by public sector accountability moves stemming from the Financial Management Initiative, while many more are affected indirectly through the spread of the contract culture to those central and local government departments which fund or purchase services from charities. And nearly all charities are significantly affected by new regulations on annual reports, annual accounts, audit and independent examination which at the time of writing (January 1995) are subject to consultation between charities, charity advisers and the Voluntary Services Unit of the Home Office. Nevertheless, some conclusions are suggested from the survey of reporting practices referred to in the Appendix, and these are the subject of this chapter.

Management reporting

The comment by the NCVO (1990) working party report on effectiveness in charities that 'great emphasis has been placed on the need for charities to be more accountable to the outside world' certainly still rings true. But so does the comment that 'there has been surprisingly little discussion about the need to improve internal management reporting techniques' and that 'if an organisation is seeking to improve its efficiency and effectiveness, it should first look at its own internal flow of management information'.

The ICSA Charities Management series of books, of which this is one, does seek to address this weakness, and there are several research projects under way which will throw further light in this area. Some of the findings from my own research are likely to be overtaken by events and by subsequent more rigorous research enquiries. Even so, the overall conclusion of my own enquiries is that the charity sector is lagging behind both the private sector, where management accountants have always been greatly concerned with performance measurement, and the public sector, which has recently been inundated with performance-measurement initiatives.

Ultimate responsibility for the performance of a charity rests with its trustees. In order properly to monitor operational performance, trustees should meet formally on a regular basis. Monthly meetings would seem appropriate, and this is the norm for directors' meetings in the corporate sector. Even small charities with few transactions might be expected to hold formal meetings to monitor events not less than quarterly, since unless there is a regular monitoring procedure it is difficult to keep an eye on trends or to identify an adverse change or omission in the charity's transactions. According to the small survey referred to in the Appendix to this book, a quarter of managers met with trustees to consider financial results less often than four times a year, and in the case of small charities the lower quartile of managers surveyed met only twice a year.

When results are considered, most appear to have regard to budgeted income and expenditure statements. Since budgets are a major aspect of performance measurement this is an encouraging finding, even if, as is no doubt the case, the quality of budget preparation varies widely.

Income and expenditure accounts should not be considered in isolation. It is very easy for income and expenditure to be incorrectly calculated or even to be deliberately manipulated, and a balance sheet is some safeguard against error, especially if the basis of the figures, their verification and any unexpected changes, is questioned critically.

An understanding of the balance sheet is also required for a review of reserve levels, to review the status of restricted or endowment funds, and as a start to cash-flow forecasts. It is of some concern that the sample showed that most charities do not present a balance sheet to their trustees when interim financial results are reviewed. As a matter of good practice and financial accounting discipline, trustees should expect a balance sheet to accompany income and expenditure accounts (or the new statement of financial activities in the future if applicable).

Though a budget comparison with actual income or expenditure figures is helpful, the significance of many figures can only be appreciated where they are expressed as a ratio of some sort. This is particularly so in the case of performance measures. In the sample of charities surveyed, the majority, even in the case of larger charities, claimed not to make regular use of any financial ratios. It would be good practice for trustees to identify selected key financial ratios appropriate to their charity for regular monitoring. Ratios of funds raised to fund-raising expenditure, proportion of income expended on charitable purposes, returns on funds invested are examples – but key ratios will vary greatly according to circumstances.

In charities particularly, many performance measures are not financial and budgets alone may often not be relevant. More than half the charities responding to the survey claimed to consider non-financial performance indicators regularly. It is good practice to ensure that outputs, such as client attendances or number of deliveries, are regularly recorded and monitored, and this seems to be the most common type of non-financial performance measure. A number of charities also regularly monitor their inputs, in the form of staff or volunteer numbers, for example. Again, input and output measures alone are insufficient to assess efficiency and effectiveness, so some important ratios of output to input, such as clients satisfactorily placed as a proportion of clients referred, or clients interviewed per volunteer hour, should be considered. It would be good practice for trustees to consider how they can monitor economy, efficiency and effectiveness and to develop a menu of ratios to be reviewed regularly to this end.

Most respondents to the survey of charities thought that their trustees were able to judge whether the performance of the charity was improving or not. At least a quarter of the small and medium charities' respondents thought otherwise, but the basis of this judgement seemed rather tenuous in nearly all cases. Several responded that no single measure was sufficient, and this is clearly the case. Even so, trustees should be able to choose a few performance indicators which would allow them to form a judgement on performance and to strive for continuous improvement. In many cases the judgement about performance seems to be made on the basis of 'feel' and is not quantified.

There is some evidence that economies of scale lead to higher efficiency in larger charities, which would suggest that smaller charities should cooperate in joint ventures or mergers. Some three-quarters of charities surveyed reported some loose arrangements for cooperation or information-sharing with another charity or charities, though only 20% went so far as to compare performance. There is nevertheless a high degree of interest in exploring opportunities for best-practice benchmarking, and this seems to present a way for charities to assess their performance and to seek improvements.

Summary of main findings

Performance measures are needed to allow the charity sector to justify its existence to the public at large and to the government of the day. Unless performance measures are in place, it is difficult for the sector as a whole to counter criticisms or for individual charities to refute accusations of poor management and ineffectiveness.

Measurement is essential to the process of management. The management aphorism 'What gets measured gets done' expresses the fact that measurement enables and motivates managers to take effective action. Similarly, the concept of continuous improvement, which is central to total quality management, cannot be applied without defining and measuring performance.

Rational management decisions and controls require good knowledge of the objectives of an organisation and also of the comparative effects of alternative actions available to meet the objectives. Because of the number of different interests in some charities it is not always easy to reach consensus about objectives, nor is it easy in many charitable areas to compare the costs and benefits of alternative actions available. Managements wishing to demonstrate that they are giving value for money and that they are making good use of the resources under their control do, therefore, have to make a conscious effort to establish agreed aims and to measure the inputs and outputs of the processes under their control.

Audited accounts are backward-looking by their nature. They are intended to serve the interests of accountability. Management needs to have forward-looking information. In this management context, past accounts are relevant only for reviewing what has happened and for setting future plans within a framework of trends and previous experience. Many of the arguments about accountability in the charity sector seem to confuse these roles. The NCVO (1990) working party on effectiveness in the sector concluded that in the recent and prolonged debate about the need to improve financial management in charities, there has been great emphasis on external accountability and relatively little discussion on how to improve internal management information. In particular, it recommended management tools such as strategic plans, annual budgets, regular management information reporting variances between actual and budget, and the production of a mission statement. These matters have been considered in this book.

The overall purpose of a business is to make a proper return on its capital employed, and most business ratios can be related to this primary ratio. Charities do not have such a common aim, and without it there is no single ratio which can be used to encapsulate overall performance or to compare the performance of one charity with that of another. Assessing performance in a charity is a complex task requiring consideration of both financial and non-financial results. Assessment is best made by separate consideration of the three Es – economy, efficiency and effectiveness – where economy denotes providing resources at the least cost consistent with the objectives; efficiency means maximising outputs relative to resources; and effectiveness measures the degree to which outputs achieve the results intended. In an organisation seeking to maximise profitability, efficiency must be the principal concern; charities by their nature pursue ends which do not have a direct economic payback, and for them effectiveness should be the principal concern.

The concepts of value for money – the three Es – imply a comparison or relationship between two factors. Performance indicators should reflect this by being in the form of ratios of some sort. They may be financial (such as direct expenditure on charitable objects as a proportion of income received) or non-financial (such as the proportion of hostel bed spaces occupied); both these examples are input/output ratios indicating efficiency.

It is helpful also to consider performance measurement from the perspective of the various stakeholders concerned. Beneficiaries of charities require special consideration because they are usually unable to exercise any power and there is always a danger that their interests will be subordinated to those with more power in the organisation. At the same time, the donors who make the operations of the charity possible must also be considered, for their wishes establish the trust funds and must be respected to avoid any breach of trust.

Performance needs to be assessed at both the strategic and the operational levels. Naturally, strategic performance can only be assessed over a long-time period when it provides feedback to the strategic planning process, whereas operational performance requires constant monitoring when it allows management control to be exercised.

Operational performance depends on the establishment of objectives. Objectives in turn are derived from a strategic view of what a charity should be doing to bring about the alleviation of needs which it has recognised. This strategic view is expressed as a mission statement or statement of purpose. The mission statement is derived from the legal objects of the charity but is a management statement rather than a legal one. It should require total commitment by senior managers and set attitudes which will permeate the whole organisation.

The mission statement is ideally supported by a statement of values to which the charity and those who work with it subscribe. This assists in reinforcing goal congruence within the organisation and in maintaining motivation among volunteers.

The mission statement is usually a general strategic affirmation. To be useful for operational planning and control purposes is has to be translated into quantified objectives – objectives which are smart, that is, *s*pecific, *m*easurable, *a*chievable, *r*elevant and *t*ime-related. This translation process, through mission to means to measures, means that the overall mission needs to be analysed first into key performance areas or critical success factors vital to the achievement of the mission.

From the critical success factors it is possible to derive divisional or departmental objectives out of which action plans may be developed and quantified in financial terms as budgets for formal approval. Individual work programmes and objectives may be derived from the divisional objectives within agreed action plans and budgets. In this way the strategic aims of the organisation are converted through the objectives cascade into increasingly specific operational targets and budgets for control. At the end of the process there should be clearly defined strategies and operational objectives for each function and activity.

Having agreed objectives, systems should be reviewed to make sure that the charity can capture information on inputs and outputs. It is the relationship between inputs, outputs and objectives which allows proper judgements about performance to be made.

Inputs are commonly recorded in value terms; charities are, indeed, bound to keep proper records to show what they have spent their money on. Inputs should also be recorded in non-financial terms, such as volunteer days or hostel bed/days, where the inputs are significant to operations, especially if the input supply is a limiting factor in the operations of the charity. Finance is itself frequently a limiting factor, and for that reason performance indicators are certain to include cost ratios and the ratio of charitable expenditure to income available.

Performance measurement presupposes a good costing system, and this requirement has been underlined recently by the move towards contracting, whereby public services are deliverable by charities in return for payments based on the service level agreed and delivered instead of, as was more usually the case, on a general grant.

Charities should take advice on costing systems if necessary and, when negotiating contract prices, need to understand the effects of volume changes on costs and the fact that prices must reflect an appropriate element of overhead. Managers should attempt to ensure that government or grant-giving trusts appreciate the cost structure of the charity which they support.

Charities' outputs are likely to be best expressed in non-financial measures. These may not be automatically produced by the charities' accounting systems, and special procedures may have to be introduced to collect the statistics.

Outputs express the product of the activities, which should in turn promote desired outcomes. Outputs by definition should be capable of quantification, whereas outcomes may be less precisely measurable and more remote from the direct influence of the charitable activities. Measuring outputs is essential to the process of assessing operational performance, whereas measuring outcomes can be less frequently undertaken as part of a strategic review process.

From a consideration of objectives, inputs and outputs, trustees should design measures of performance relevant to the organisation and to each manager whose performance is to be monitored. It is not possible to suggest a set of indicators common to all charities, but the aim should be to select a small range of measures, probably more than five but not more than ten for any manager, in the form of ratios, including ratios covering economy, efficiency and effectiveness.

Procedures should encourage economy by requiring any major item of expenditure to be subject to tender; products or services should be designed to avoid unnecessary cost, that is, any cost which does not ultimately add benefit by means of value analysis; and accounting or administrative systems should be designed to identify and to combat fraud and waste. A rolling cost review of all significant spending and regular comparison of costs with those obtaining elsewhere should be part of these processes.

The principal measure of operational efficiency will normally be expressed in terms of the key outputs per unit of key input. At the higher level, a suitable indicator of efficiency is the amount of money spent on charitable causes as a proportion of the total money collected, but this indicator, like any other, should not be used in isolation. At lower levels it is often better to use physical rather than financial measures. Procedures should ensure control of scarce resources – spare land, unbanked cash, and any human resource surplus, for example.

Measuring effectiveness is of the greatest difficulty in a charity. A charity's aims are more important than mere economic or financial aims, so neither objectives nor outputs may be financially quantifiable. Where it is possible to use proxy measures, such as opportunity costs, to assess the value of outputs, this should be done. Usually, however, it is important for trustees to devise ways of measuring outputs in non-financial terms which they can compare with the objectives which they have established for their charity. Quality should be tested, where possible, by carrying out client surveys on a sample basis – for example, student feedback questionnaires in an educational environment.

Budgets are traditionally thought of as financial management tools, but they are more than that. Budgets are an integral part of the planning and control systems and need to be adapted to serve the purposes of performance measurement. Charities are accustomed to using budgets. It is a small step, therefore, to seek improvements in budget techniques as a way to improve performance measurement in charities.

Recent developments in budgeting make them particularly relevant to charities – the increasing inclusion in budgets of non-financial measures, the importance of specifying outputs and not just cost inputs, the emphasis on activity- and priority-based budget methods, and the use of budgets in controlling overhead expenditure. Zero-base budgeting methods have important benefits for charities: they require managers to justify budgets on the basis of agreed objectives which are aligned to the overall mission for the charity; and they make no assumptions as to continued funding from year to year.

Zero-base budgeting methods are particularly supportive in a performance-measurement context because each manager must define unit objectives, specify inputs, consider processes and define quantifiable outputs. This provides all the ingredients for value-for-money review and for establishing performance measures relevant to each manager.

Recent research indicates that the proportion of income used directly for charitable purposes is higher in large than in smaller charities; and conversely, that administration takes a lower proportion of total income in large charities than in smaller ones. It may be suggested that there are too many charities operating and that the sector would benefit from some rationalisation. There is scope for more mergers and for cooperative and cost-sharing ventures in the charity sector.

Meanwhile, the existence of so many charities provides an opportunity for the assessment of performance using comparisons between them. Charities should make greater use of best-practice benchmarking as a means of comparing operational performance with the best practices elsewhere in the sector or outside it. Benchmarking is a way of assessing performance in key process areas by reference to others who are examples of best practice in that field. It is a joint cooperative exercise which requires the friendly participation of both parties with a view to achieving continuous improvements in performance. The links with commerce and industry by way of sponsorships and donations should be further developed by benchmarking partnerships.

Performance measurement is often thought of as a short-term control mechanism concerned with measuring operational performance on a day-to-day, or at least on a month-to-month, basis. Alongside the operational performance-measurement systems, however, trustees should also ensure that a strategic performance measurement review system is in place. The strategic performance-measurement system does not require such frequent monitoring and cannot be applied with such detailed and accurate measures as the operational system. But the strategic review of performance is ultimately more important because it reaffirms (or not as the case may be) the mission of the charity and the way in which the mission is implemented.

Strategic review of performance should involve a balanced view of stakeholder perspectives and activities within the charity. A model linking these includes three external perspectives (those of the beneficiaries; the public and those who provide funds directly; and the government which provides funds on the public's behalf) and three internal aspects of the charity's work (the charity workers themselves; the processes in the charity whereby value is provided to beneficiaries; and the reserves which exist within the charity).

Of the strategic review areas, the primary one is concerned with the perspective of the beneficiaries – those persons or objects for whom the charity was established and continues to exist. The review should redefine the extent of the need which the charity seeks to address, and it should review the objectives of the charity, that is, the means by which the needs are addressed. It will have been assumed that the means selected will lead to satisfactory outcomes which meet to some extent the needs identified. The strategic review should consider the appropriateness of outcomes relative to needs and the relevance of the chosen means to the outcomes.

The strategic review should cover the ability of the charity to attract funds, having regard to the charity's public image, its relationship with the government, and its own reserves. A charity should establish a reserves policy as part of its strategic planning and performance-measurement policy.

Within the strategic review of performance, the charity should plan the relationship between trustees, paid staff and volunteer workers, as well as the way in which workers are motivated and rewarded and how their performance should be monitored. It should also examine the processes carried out to ensure that they remain appropriate and that they are carried out efficiently.

10 Case studies

National Association for Children without a Home

Synopsis

This case study is based on an actual project but with modifications to suit the points illustrated; the circumstances described are no longer applicable. The case concerns a charity organised on a national basis. It had grown quite rapidly both by adding functions and by establishing regional offices. The departmental heads were allowed considerable authority; in some cases they maintained their own bank accounts, and regional offices resented interference from head office. Financial control was seen as a low-level function subordinate to the real task of improving child care. The charity had traditionally been supported by government grants which provided about a third of the total income, the rest being derived from membership subscriptions, fees for services and donations. The government wishes to assure itself that value for money is provided before committing more grant aid.

Background

The charity was formed in the 1950s to coordinate and support the work of the large number of local voluntary adoption societies which became members. Membership was later extended to local authorities. In 1980 the charity merged with another charity which existed to find families for children.

In the 1980s there were almost 200 adoption agencies, of which 60% were local authorities, in the charity's regions:

	Agencies	Children in care
South London	16	5,051
North London	28	6,169
S.W. England	12	3,820
S.E. England	19	7,566
Wales	11	3,593
East Anglia	9	4,209
Midlands	24	13,350
North West	25	10,694
Yorkshire and Humberside	19	7,215
North	15	4,831
England and Wales	178	66,498

The charity had been supported by government grants. It was calculated that in the mid 1980s the cost of keeping a child in care was over £350 per week.

Objectives

The charity's objects include:

- bringing together children needing care with families able to provide care;
- establishing good standards of practice among agencies;
- acting as a central source of information on the needs of children for homes;
- promoting public and professional understanding of the issues involved.

There has been a major change since the 1960s as there are now few babies for adoption relative to those wishing to adopt and the main difficulty is in finding homes for children with special needs. The charity's exchange service is designed to address this need. It placed over 100 children in 1978 and over 200 in 1988.

Organisation

The charity is managed by trustees through a full-time director to whom the following report directly:

membership/computer officer
administrator (reception and office services)
appeals officer
financial accountant
exchange service director
assistant director northern regions
assistant director southern regions
assistant director development, to whom report
   social worker enquiry officer
   medical group secretary
   legal group secretary
   racial issues project leader
   publications officer
   press and information officer

The main functions may be classified as follows:

* the exchange service, including production of the *Make a Home* catalogue;
* training and consultancy work for professionals designed to raise standards;
* publishing and communicating knowledge designed to influence the public and public authorities;
* fund-raising and appeals work;
* administration, including accounting, personnel, building and equipment management and membership.

The exchange function and the training consultancy function require personal interface with professionals on the ground. A network of eight regional centres has been developed, each of which should have at least one exchange officer and one trainer/consultant.

Staff may be classified as follows:

	HQ	Regions	Total
Exchange services	5	11	16
Professional support and development	12	10	22
Publications, PR and fund-raising	8	1	9
Administration, finance, data processing, membership and secretarial	14	15	29
Total staffing	39	37	76

Exchange service

The exchange service is controlled from head office, but data input and output facilities are used by regional offices. Details of approved families and parentless children are available to all regions. Agencies referring a child pay a referral fee and on successful linking a placement fee is charged. Volumes are as follows:

	Children referred	Children placed	Fees earned (£'000)
1985	273	155	155
1986	329	141	171
1987	459	211	217
1988	615	235	274

Make a Home magazine is designed to encourage parents to come forward to adopt or foster. The editor wishes to promote greater media coverage which it is believed would generate more placements and higher income.

Training/consultancy

Training is conducted from both head office and regional offices. Fees are charged based on time on site plus preparation time. Head office issued 65 invoices in 1988/89. They are issued by the training officer, who records them in a register which is used in completing VAT returns, but there is no record in the financial accounts until cash is received and paid in. The auditors have previously drawn attention to the fact that invoices issued often remain unpaid and have to be written off. There is more demand for training and consultancy than the organisation can currently meet.

The head office training manager also organises national seminars, of which there were eight in 1989 with an average attendance of 180 and an expected income of £9,900 per seminar.

Research and liaison

The social worker enquiry officer handled 555 written enquiries in 1988, of which 142 were from outside the UK. In addition, there were many telephone enquiries, which are not logged.

Much time is spent in organising interdisciplinary meetings and in liaison with adoption agencies and professionals in the area. The department also commissions or carries out research projects, though there has been insufficient income to fund research in recent years.

There seems no suitable way in which these services can charge fees for enquiries and for liaison work.

Publications are charged for, except that some are issued free to subscribing members and some, such as promotional leaflets and annual accounts, are issued free of charge on request. Present accounting systems make it difficult to measure the commercial success of the publications section.

Appeals

The appeals officer has an assistant and shared secretarial support. The aim is to produce income which is four times the cost of salaries and promotional costs. The appeals officer targets charitable trusts to provide two-thirds of appeals income and major companies to provide about a fifth.

Accounting and finance

The finance officer is a qualified accountant but has no computer experience. He has recently been given one assistant but nevertheless has a heavy workload and also looks after health and safety matters and building maintenance administration. Payroll is handled by a bureau, but accounting records are manual. Regional officers and some head office departments send monthly returns of income and expenditure by post which are used to complete the accounting records.

A computer manager looks after membership records in the form of data-base records on a PC. He also supervises use of three head office PCs which provide word-processing facilities and handle the records of the adoption exchange service.

Budgets are prepared each year for approval by the management committee but are not phased by months so that interim comparisons between actual and budget are difficult. Also, because income is generated and expenditure incurred by regions and other head office departments which do not always report promptly, the quarterly accounts, prepared on a cash basis, do not always reflect the true income and expenditure position, and a balance sheet is not prepared until the year end. Audited accounts are often materially different from the management accounts. At the last year end regional bank balances totalled some £35,000, while head office accounts showed an overdrawn position of some £50,000.

Audit reports have drawn attention to weaknesses in controlling receipts, the absence of an up-to-date asset register, and problems with the stock and creditor records. Their latest report states that:

little liaison between the various departments for the purpose of identifying and following up significant overdue balances . . . may result in debtors who owe large amounts to the organisation: a substantial amount of time is spent producing invoices for customers who frequently fail to pay.

In the last audited accounts a deficit arose on the general fund account which had to be financed from special restricted funds.

Required

(a) The government department which supports the activity of the charity by means of grants has asked for your views on whether value for money is being achieved. How would you approach this task? Suggest output and performance measures which would be appropriate. How might you distinguish outputs and outcomes? What sort of strategic review might be appropriate? Would it be more appropriate to support the charity by contract payments or by core-fund grant?

(b) How would you recommend that the director should amend the organisation structure and institute improved planning processes?

(c) In view of criticisms of the financial control systems, recommend actions which you think are most important to improve control.

(d) Explain to the financial accountant how he might benefit from learning to use a spreadsheet package on one of the PCs, and give examples of some of the uses to which it could be put. Are there other training needs appropriate to the accountant?

(e) What reports should the trustees call for and what timetable would be suitable? What statements should accompany the usual income and expenditure accounts?

(f) The exchange services manager has requested that a sum of £20,000 be spent on promotion to increase awareness of the scheme. Market research shows that this greater level of awareness would identify more suitable parents who would adopt. This would result in increased fee earning, but because of the time taken by adoption proceedings and delays in payment cash receipts would be delayed. Extra cash receipts are expected as follows:

Years after spend	£
1	4,000
2	10,000
3	8,000
4	2,000
Total	24,000

The financial accountant recommends this on the grounds that the cost would be repaid before three years and overall a return of 20% would be earned. The charity's investments earn about 8% p.a. How should this investment decision be approached?

Association for the Study of Drug Dependence Limited

Background

The ASDD is a company limited by guarantee and formed for charitable purposes. Its objectives are:

• to collect, collate, interpret and disseminate information on all aspects of drug dependence;

- to establish and maintain a reference library and information-retrieval system;
- to promote and undertake research into the causes, prevention and treatment of drug dependence;
- to arrange lectures, discussions and seminars, including international conferences;
- to cooperate with other bodies, both national and international, in furthering the study of drug dependence;
- generally to provide a centre for the study, and to advance public understanding, of drug dependence by all appropriate means.

The ASDD owns the freehold of its offices in central London but it also rents nearby office accommodation since it has insufficient space for its existing staff and records. The work of ASDD is complementary to more direct work in the drugs field by other charities dealing with drug and alcohol abuse.

The organisation is divided into three operating units – the library/information unit; the publications unit; and the research and development unit – which are serviced by a fourth unit handling administration and fund-raising.

The library/information unit has two joint heads of department. It collects abstracts and files data from the English-speaking world. It answers questions arriving by post or telephone usually by sending a reference list or by inviting the enquirer to come to the library. Enquiries are free, but if any volume of photocopying is required a charge of 20p per page is levied. Four publications are distributed monthly to subscribers who pay £20 per year. Enquiries run at about 9,000 per year. The information base is large, and 200 items are added each month.

The publications unit handles books and pamphlets sold by ASDD, and produces the regular bimonthly magazine *Infodrug*. This unit, too, has joint heads of department. The circulation of *Infodrug* has doubled to 1,200 since its recent introduction. It is provided free to members and sold separately to others.

The research and development unit undertakes projects which are externally funded, typically by research trusts or government agencies requiring reports or educational materials. The unit hopes to cover direct costs and make a small contribution to general overheads.

The administration unit is controlled by the deputy director, who, like the other heads of department, reports to the director, who forms the link between the operating units and the governing body, the Council. This unit covers administration, accounting and finance, personnel and fund-raising activities.

Unit heads do not receive management accounts for their units but they control their own staff, who are on the Association of University Teachers' (AUT) pay scales, and do their own invoicing for any work done or publications supplied. Monthly accounts are produced for the whole organisation which show:

	Government grant £000	Other income £000
1989	158	361
1990	184	395
1991	240	464

The business has more or less broken even each year, so that expenditure is equal to the income and grant columns above. In 1991 expenditure was as follows:

	£000
Salaries	371
Direct costs	129
General overheads	204

Funding arrangements are on an annual basis at present, and there are practically no reserves, so that the operations are particularly dependent on current cash flow. The freehold premises are at an old valuation of £220,000 but should realise twice that figure if sold.

The sponsoring government department has recently reviewed the ASDD and is keen to move to longer-term financing arrangements with less reliance on departmental grants, but has criticised the lack of financial management information and planning. As a result of the review the director has appointed you as financial adviser, and the previous deputy director has taken early retirement.

Required

The director asks you:

(a) to draft a paper for the Council explaining why it might be beneficial to prepare a five-year plan for the organisation. Prepare an outline report setting out
  (i) the advantages of completing a long-term planning exercise;
  (ii) how you propose to set about preparing the plan and what it will contain;
  (iii) any involvement you may request from the Council.

(b) to make recommendations to him for establishing a management reporting and performance measurement system to be implemented as soon as the plan is approved. Prepare your report with recommendations, and reasons, on the sort of information to be provided and to whom the information should be made available.

(c) to advise him on the proposal to invest in labour-saving equipment. The head of the publications department wishes to acquire a new desktop publishing system with printers and automatic folding and ancillary equipment which would greatly improve the ability to produce the magazine *Infodrug*. The equipment will cost £95,000, and as a result it will be possible to reduce staffing requirements by two part-time assistants who currently cost £6,000 per year. The department is willing to authorise such expenditure provided a real return on capital of 5% can be demonstrated. The equipment should have an effective life of ten years, by which time it is likely to be worthless. Employment costs are expected to increase by 5% each year, although the department assumes a general rate of inflation of only 4%. Show the calculations you would make to evaluate the proposal financially, and show whether the proposal should be approved or, if not, at what cost the proposed equipment could be justified. Explain to the head of department the method you have used to evaluate his proposal and why, and draw attention to any assumptions or non-financial considerations to be borne in mind when making the decision.

North London Rehabilitation Centre

You are approached by the chairman of a board of directors/ trustees of a small charity formed in 1991/92 to provide work for mentally handicapped people in three north London boroughs. The directors are mainly occupational therapist professionals attached to the area's mental hospital.

The charity believes that work demands the exercise of individual responsibility, the toleration of frustrations and the exercise of sensory and perceptual judgement. It provides a correspondence between perception and reality, opportunities for achievement, sense of purpose and self-esteem, and a structure for social interaction outside a family or institutional environment. Work is thus a major tool in the treatment and rehabilitation of clients with mental health problems.

In order to provide work the charity has formed its own printshop to do small print runs and photocopying for customers, both members of the public and local businesses. It also has a catering kitchen which prepares meals for staff and clients and in addition provides sandwiches for local offices and for the hospital shop. More recently a laundry has been opened and a contract cleaning and gardening service has been started. The charity charges competitive prices, but the rate of clients' work is slow and the charity's costs exceed the income, the shortfall being made up by local government grants.

The charity was formed as a company and has grown well but over recent years there have been increasingly acrimonious disagreements between the board and its general manager. At the last board meeting the inability to work together came to a head and the general manager was removed from her position despite her good commercial knowledge and popularity with the staff.

The chairman calls in some urgency: the end of the financial year is imminent. He provides a latest statement of expected receipts and payments; a draft budget has been prepared by the general manager but not discussed with the unit managers nor yet approved by the trustees (the copy of the budget, which he attaches, has only financial information and consists of one summary of all the accounts to show the balance between income and expenditure for the charity as a whole); and the bookkeeper who remains has a poor understanding of the financial position and accounting requirements.

The chairman explains that the charity provides work for about 70 workers (rehabilitation clients) as shown by the latest attendance register (which was attached for the current month and shows daily how many sessions of each work placement are attended by clients).

He has an establishment of eight staff:

- general manager – position to be filled temporarily by new manager with occupational therapy and some business experience;
- catering manager – also deputy general manager, responsible particularly for meals for workers and organising catering services to public and to local hospital cafés;
- café supervisor – based at local hospital;
- contract cleaning manager – managing contracts for cleaning services to premises in the borough;
- print manager – managing printing and photocopying facilities for the public and local businesses;
- laundry supervisor – managing laundry services to the public;
- administration officer and bookkeeper;
- clerical supervisor – managing clerical/secretarial work for the public and local businesses.

He is concerned to establish a business plan for the charity and to put in place some information system to monitor the performance of the charity.

(a) What further information will you seek to collect initially?
(b) How would you recommend that the budget statements be set out and what costing principles would you bear in mind?
(c) What actions should be taken to prepare a business plan?
(d) What measures of performance should be put in place?
(e) What procedures would be recommended for the collection and communication of performance measures?

East Regional Association for the Deaf (ERAD)

Synopsis

This case is based on an actual investigation but names, client benefit groups and circumstances are changed. The charity has a defined geographical area of operation covering roughly half of England; another charity deals with the other half of the country. The two organisations talk together from time to time in an informal way but are jealous to protect their own independence and cultures.

Background

The charity was formed at the beginning of this century. Its formal objectives are 'the promotion of the welfare of the deaf and those substantially permanently handicapped by defective hearing, and the prevention of deafness'. The last annual report restates the aim as to ensure a better quality of life for all auditively impaired people and to prevent hearing impairment.

The aims are dealt with through four sub-committees with objectives as follows:

- deaf and other handicaps – to improve the quality of life of deaf people with additional handicaps;
- employment – to advance equal opportunities for people with hearing impairment;
- training – to ensure that the training and support available for those involved in meeting the needs of those with hearing impairment is comprehensive, up-to-date and of high quality in order to provide the best service to those with hearing impairment;
- medical – to ensure that no person's hearing is unnecessarily impaired.

In practice, most of the charity's resources are concentrated on training, and the charity has received substantial government funding to this end. The charity has four general staff, the general secretary and her assistant, a part-time accountant and a part time librarian, and eight training staff comprising a training supervisor, a training administrator and six trainers.

The charity is managed by an executive committee which has five sub-committees:

- finance and general purposes, meeting quarterly;
- employment, meeting quarterly;

- training, meeting half-yearly;
- deaf/disabled, meeting half yearly; and
- medical, meeting annually.

The charity has cash and investments totalling some £66,000 and current liabilities of £30,000, leaving £36,000 in the general fund. Income and expenditure are as follows:

Income	
Training fees	26,000
Investment income	6,000
Affiliation fees	1,000
Deficit financed by government grant	124,000
Total	157,000
Expenditure	
Administration	67,000
Occupancy costs	12,000
Communications	12,000
Training costs	66,000
Total	157,000

Training costs above are only direct costs of training; much of the administrative, occupancy and communications costs are also attributable to training activities. Grants are agreed annually and the charity does not see any point in preparing long-term plans, given the short-term nature of grant support.

The charity keeps records of candidates attending the training courses and it has been possible to calculate the number of candidate training days in the year as 5,030. This, together with the fact that most courses are fully booked, is quoted as evidence that value for money is provided.

The charity also claims that it is competitive with its sister charity in the other half of England and Wales because several authorities in the other half choose to send their officers to the charity for training rather than to their own region. The sister charity's response is that the subject charity receives a higher degree of government subsidy and can thus offer courses more cheaply – in short, the competition is unfair and a consequence of flawed government funding policies.

The central government department responsible for funding would like to encourage longer-term arrangements than the current annual negotiated settlement but the charities fear that without larger reserves they may be unable to maintain continuity. Half the government grants are at present borne by local authorities, but some refuse to pay and their costs are in practice added to the costs of those who do pay.

After investigations have been carried out you obtain statistics from the sister charity, the West Regional Association for the Deaf (WRAD), and from a third organisation providing a national service from a subsidiary operation financed out of its own, larger charitable resources. These are compared with those of the ERAD in Table 10.1. These three operations together provide all training for recognised workers with deaf people in England and Wales.

Required

(a) Are the objectives appropriate to the charity's work? Could they be improved as a basis for objective setting and value-for-money analysis?

(b) What performance measures might be developed to indicate economy, efficiency and effectiveness? and

(c) What means could be adopted to assess the performance measures chosen?

(d) What are the advantages and disadvantages of deficit funding:
    (i)   for the charity; and
    (ii) for the government?

One plus One

This case consists of extracts from an article in *The Times* by Julia Llewellyn Smith (1995). The article starts with comments on the background of Dr Jack Dominian and how he met and fell in love with his wife. It continues:

For nearly 25 years, his mission, as the founder of the charity One plus One, has been to investigate not why couples divorce, but why they stay together. Last year he was appointed MBE for his services to the institution; now he has published his findings in *Marriage*, billed rather

Table 10.1 ERAD comparative statistics

	ERAD	WRAD	Hearing centre
Expenditure budget	£	£	£
Training			
Salaries and superannuation	50,300	74,635	160,500
Tutor training and support cost	8,900	19,500	21,800
Occupancy	2,950	–	75,700
Travel and communications	3,500	500	22,500
Administrative costs			30,200
Total	65,650	94,635	310,700
Administration			
Administrative and clerical costs	67,700	105,360	
Occupancy	12,050	37,185	
Communications	12,100	23,800	
Total costs	**157,500**	**260,980**	**310,700**
Less income			
Fees charged	26,000	59,000	40,000
Affiliation fees	1,155	800	
Investment income	6,100	2,600	
Grant required	**124,245**	**198,580**	**270,700**
Central government	62,123	99,290	
Local government	62,122	99,290	
Grant making charity			270,700
Staff–FTE	no	no	no
Total	8.5	12	10
Trainers	5.5	7	6
Salary of most senior manager (£)	22,100	17,900	24,500
Fees charged – typical examples	£	£	£
Rehab worker cert course short course	1,800	3,550	4,200
associate	free	70	100
others	150	140	100
Candidate course days	5,030	2,965	1,523
Number of registered deaf or partially deaf in the region	68,907	122,261	

ambitiously by his publishers as 'The definitive guide to what makes a marriage work'.

The article then discusses his qualifications and record:

educated at Cambridge and Oxford; a senior consultant psychiatrist since 1965, 15 books (with titles such as *Christian Marriage*); a 40-year marriage to his wife, by whom he has four daughters. The article describes his wife as smiling and friendly which is more than can be said for her husband, who reluctantly comes downstairs saying 'I Don't like publicity very much. I like writing books.'

Nonetheless, he needs the publicity, not only for himself but for his organisation which, he claims, is woefully underfunded. All we are putting into marriage-related charities is two to three million pounds. Meanwhile, says Dr Dominian, 40 per cent of British marriages end in divorce, costing the taxpayer at least £3 billion a year, in terms of social security, police, court and prison expenses, lost production and NHS costs. His book produces statistics to show that children whose parents stay together – however miserably – stand a greater chance of happiness than those whose parents split up . . .

The article quotes Dr Dominian:

There are only two things in life which give us the majority of our contentment. One is work and one is marital life, and I would rate marital life as the most important. It fulfils a certain number of basic human needs: attachment, bonding, intimacy, love, sex. There's no other institution that can make comprehensive provision for all of this.

After discussing briefly why things go wrong the doctor is quoted again:

Once marriage was a contract of social roles. Now we expect much greater emotional and sexual fulfilment. We want egalitarian, loving relationships, and this is not in itself a bad thing. We just don't know how to develop it.

Dr Dominian's intention is that we should be taught such useful advice in personal educational programmes in schools.

We take a lot of trouble learning to drive a car. We have to take a lot of trouble learning about contemporary marriage. We have to take it much more seriously and learn that when problems come we will have to work at them . . . People are not promiscuous. We are shaped for love from the moment when we are born. We want to capture that bond with our mother from the cradle to the grave.

On the basis of this brief article, consider the following questions:

(a) How might the charity address the six-point strategic review described in Chapter 8? How might it address public and government relations to advance its cause? Are large internal reserves likely to be necessary and what processes and support should the charity require?
(b) How successful would you think that the charity has been in translating the vision of Dr Dominian into a mission and into actionable objectives? Would such a charity be more effective acting alone or as part of a larger charity grouping?
(c) What outputs might be appropriate and how might they be quantified and measured? What outcomes are desirable, how might they be measured and what difficulties might be experienced in relating outputs to outcomes?

Cases review

National Association for Children without a Home and Association for the Study of Drug Dependence Limited

Both these cases raise the question of the interaction between organisation and performance measurement. The first, in particular, highlights problems which can arise if performance measurement does not seem to be treated seriously by senior management. In the second there is some lack of clarity about responsibilities for performance. The organisation should be designed to ensure that each budget centre is the clear responsibility of a budget centre manager with defined ouput targets as well as expenditure budgets.

Output measures are not easy to determine, but the case of the National Association for Children without a Home gives some clue as to the use of proxy output values to demonstrate value for money and perhaps to guide the value of contract fees for future service level agreements.

Both charities are based in central London. How does this location impact on economy and effectiveness? Does London weighting allowance in pay scales provide any basis for assessing measures of economy?

In each of these case studies a capital expenditure problem was raised. This is not discussed at length in the book, which tends to dismiss return on capital as a performance measure. Where capital is a limiting factor, however, as is often the case, and where benefits are financial, as in these cases, it is proper to apply the same appraisal techniques as in a corporate finance situation; that is, by using discounted cash-flow methods to compare current outlays with expected future benefits.

In corporate financial management the rate of discount would theoretically be arrived at by adding to the real risk free rate of return a further rate to reflect the risk associated with the investment. There is some doubt about this approach in the not-for-profit situation but in the case of the National Association for Children without a Home the opportunity cost of capital is given as 8% which would be appropriate.

The second case study raises the question of the treatment of inflation which is ignored in the first. It is common to ignore inflation in preparing cash flows but in such a case the rate of discount should also be free of any inflation element. It is preferable to calculate cash flows to specifically include inflation and then to discount by a rate which also includes inflation. This is necessary in the second case study because the actual effect of inflation on cash flows is expected to differ from the general level of inflation. To be strictly accurate the rate of discount in this case is:

real return required	5	%
inflation rate	4	%
Fischer effect (5% × 4%)	0.2%	
Total	**9.2%**	

From a strategic point of view, there is a need to check the assumption that planned outputs do in fact lead to the desired beneficial outcomes which each charity is seeking.

North London Rehabilitation Centre

This case revolved around the budget procedures and the need to monitor the contribution made by each work activity to the fixed overheads. The charity does not expect to make a commercial profit, but it is important that the direct income from doing work should cover the variable cost of servicing that work. Unless this is the case, growth in volume of clients and work placements will simply make the deficit larger. Budget statements should enable this to be reviewed regularly. Preparation of divisional budgets and the overall budget require an understanding of the distinction between direct costs of each budget centre and indirect costs, which must be apportioned on an equitable basis across centres, and between fixed and variable costs, so that the effect of changing volumes on the overall results can be anticipated.

In this case study, the local authority negotiators attempted to argue that they should pay only the marginal costs of their rehabilitation client workers. Accepting such an argument would soon put the charity out of business. Charges must allow for some contribution to general overheads and ideally should allow some leeway for the accumulation of prudent reserves.

It is essential that workplace managers should understand and be involved in establishing their own budgets. They should be consulted on performance measures and procedures to capture the measurements.

Less frequent procedures are needed to review strategic progress towards the main aim of client rehabilitation.

East Regional Association for the Deaf

This case study provides a simple example of the opportunity to compare costs and ratios of economy, efficiency and effectiveness when there are several charities offering a comparable service in comparable circumstances. ERAD and WRAD are very similar in their activities and aims – and figures are comparable; they both have costs which can be attributed wholly to training and general costs which relate mainly to training but to other activities as well. The third organisation is less comparable; it was set up specifically for training and all costs are therefore direct costs in that sense.

In a learning situation this case study can be used for syndicate work with some taking the role of ERAD, some WRAD and some the Government role. This soon demonstrates that the choice of performance indicators often depends on the point of view from which the measurement is to be made.

Costs per trainer employed provide a measure of economy (better might be cost per training hour though trainers' time records were not maintained) and so do costs per student course day.

Course days and course fee income per trainer and per £ cost give an indication of efficiency (and also say something about the different pricing policies). It is less easy to quantify effectiveness since more needed to be known about success rates and standards.

The case also suggests fairer means of funding might be related to the service provided by contract payments, or to client needs based on the number of potential end user beneficiaries in each region, rather than the current method of negotiated deficit funding. It raises, too, the question as to whether the potential cost savings from enforcing a merger of the two related charities would offset the disadvantages of centralisation and monopoly power which a single national charity might enjoy.

One plus One

This case raises the issue of how to deal with strategies for growth. Many large and influencial charities have been established as the result of the vision of one dedicated man or woman. As a charity (or any other organisation) grows, it needs a greater range of skills and a higher degree of management. Sometimes strategies rely on internal growth. In other cases growth can be more effective with external merger/acquisition strategies. Performance measures help to monitor the success of the chosen strategies or to modify them as required.

Appendix:
Charities management
information survey

In early September 1994, 100 questionnaires were sent out to representatives of charities who had attended or expressed interest in attending South Bank Business School courses on Charity Finance. By the end of November, 57 replies had been received, three of which related to organisations which were not registered charities and which have been excluded from the analysis of the remaining 54 registered charities. It is possible that, by addressing the questionnaire to those expressing an interest in charity finance, the sample will be biased towards respondents with above average financial understanding, though there is no evidence of such bias.

The sample covered a wide range of charity sectors classified as shown in Table A.1. The size of the sample does not allow significant differences between these classes of charity to be identified, nor was there evidence of such differences. The sample was, however, subdivided into small, medium and large charities on the basis of the number of full-time equivalent staff employed, as shown in Table A.2.

Table A.1 Range of charity sectors represented in the survey

Education, training, youth	12
Social services and relief	11
Health, medicine, physical and mental handicap, age	10
Culture, sport, recreation	6
Conservation and animals	3
International	4
Business and professional	4
Religion	3
Philanthropic intermediation	1
Total sample	54

Table A.2 Breakdown of charities by size

Number of charities	Full-time equivalent staff numbers	
	Range	Mean no.
22 (small)	up to 12	5
15 (medium)	12 and under 100	41
17 (large)	100 and over	461
54		158

Respondents were asked to record how many formal head office meetings were held. The results are shown in Table A.3. As may be expected, formal meetings of managers and trustees are more frequent in larger charities. Several large charities held formal weekly management meetings and, on average, meetings of managers in large charities were twice a month, compared with monthly in medium charities and every two months for small charities.

Financial results are considered at about two-thirds of meetings, regardless of size. Trustees consider financial results quarterly in the case of small charities but twice as frequently in the case of large charities. These mean figures contain wide variations, however, as shown in Tables A.4 and A.5.

The financial information considered at formal meetings nearly always included actual income and expenditure for the relevant period, generally with comparative budget figures. Surprisingly, balance-sheet information (which is needed for a proper

Table A.3 Number of formal head office meetings held, by charity size

	No. of formal meetings		No. at which financial results were considered	
	Managers	Trustees included	Managers	Trustees included
Small	7	6	5	4
Medium	12	5	7	5
Large	20	10	11	7
All	13	7	8	5

Table A.4 Number of meetings per year at which trustees consider financial results

	Upper quartile	Median	Lower quartile
Small	4	4	2
Medium	6	4	4
Large	12	8	4
All	6	4	3

Table A.5 Number of charities reporting meetings at which trustees consider financial results

Annual frequency of meetings	Small	Medium	Large	All
Less than 4	9	4	3	16
4–7	11	10	6	27
8–11	1	1	3	5
12–16	0	0	5	5
16 and over	1	0	0	1
Total	22	15	17	54

understanding of a charity's financial position, for consideration of reserves for example, and for verification of the income and expenditure figures) is not usually considered. Cash flows are also not usually tabled but are used more frequently in smaller charities (where cash may be as useful a guide to results as an income and expenditure account, and perhaps easier for trustees to understand).

The percentage of respondents using the various financial statements in shown in Table A.6. The questionnaire asked if, in looking at financial results, any ratios were commonly considered. A surprisingly high number replied in the negative. Only 17% of small and medium-sized charities considered financial ratios, and only 47% of large charities. Of the financial ratios specified most (13) were for assessing expenditure, four related to working capital and to trading activities, four to reserve levels and to income.

Respondents were also asked whether non-financial performance indicators were commonly considered at formal meetings.

Table A.6 Use of financial statements, by size of charity (%)

	Small	Medium	Large	All
Actual income and expenditure				
Usually/always	91	100	100	96
Occasionally	5			2
Budget income and expenditure				
Usually/always	77	100	100	90
Occasionally	14	7		6
Cash-flow statements				
Usually/always	50	40	41	43
Occasionally	23	20	18	22
Balance sheet				
Usually/always	41	67	35	47
Occasionally	27	7	23	20

A majority responded positively – 50% of small charities, 73% of medium-sized charities and 75% of large charities consider some form of non-financial performance indicator. Naturally the indicators used varied greatly but, in general, the indicators were number counts showing volumes measured by clients or activity or less frequently by staff or volunteer resources. Indicators may be classified as shown in Table A.7. There were isolated examples of input/output ratios, of comparison of volumes against targets, of client satisfaction surveys and of capacity utilisation ratios, but in general the indicators measured input or output volumes rather than addressing concepts of efficiency or effectiveness.

The question 'Do you consider that your trustees are able to make a judgement on whether the performance of the charity is

Table A.7 Use of non-financial performance indicators

	Number of cases specified
Volume of output/activity	20
Number of clients/customers	16
Staff numbers (inc. turnover and human resource ratios)	7
Project evaluations/studies/audits	6
Number of volunteers	5
Unsatisfied demand/drop-out rates etc.	5
Number of members	4

improving?' generally evoked a positive response – from 75% of small charities, 67% of medium-sized charities and 88% of large charities. The supplementary question 'If so, how would you expect them to measure performance?' was less clear-cut, however. Three of the positive responses failed to suggest how performance improvement might be measured, and in many instances it was clear that the assessment of performance improvement was subjective and judgemental rather than quantifiable. Most frequently mentioned ways in which trustees would be expected to measure performance are shown in Table A.8. A number of respondents commented that there was no single measure of performance which could be used.

A few, nine out of 51, were organized on a regional basis. In these cases respondents were asked whether performance could be compared between regions and whether best- or worst-performing regions could be identified. Of the nine, seven could compare regions and six felt able to identify best or worst performance. The comparison between regions was in two cases made on the basis of actual/budget comparison but also mentioned were the number of events held, statistical data rating and satisfaction surveys.

A high proportion of all charities (73%) and and even higher proportion of large charities (88%) reported that they had agreed arrangements for cooperating with another charity or charities. Most respondents reported that the main purpose of such arrangements was the sharing of information but improvement of service quality was second, followed by the desire to reduce costs and improvement in fund-raising.

Table A.8 Ways in which trustees were expected to measure performance

	Number of cases specified
Financial results	17
Volume of output/usage	11
Qualitative judgement/observation/ verbal feedback/questions	11
Growth in income/capital/reserves	6
Delivery/output against target	5
Staff/volunteer evaluations	3

Fewer charities (20% of the total sample) reported having any arrangements to compare their performance with another organisation or organisations, and less than half of these considered this to constitute benchmarking. However, 57% of all charities and 75% of large charities reported that they would be interested in exploring opportunities for best-practice benchmarking – suggesting at least a potential demand for more comparative data and recognition of best practices in the sector.

References

Abel-Smith, B. (1976), *Value for Money in Health Services*, Heinemann

Accounting Standards Board (1995), 'Accounting by charities', *SORP 2*, final draft 1 February

Allen, D. (1995), 'Financial management', *Management Accounting* (February)

Argenti, J. (1974), *Systematic Corporate Planning*, Van Nostrand Reinhold UK

Argenti, J. (1993), *Your Organization: What is it for?*, McGraw-Hill

Audit Commission (1995), *Paying the Piper – people and pay management in local government*, HMSO

Berg, W. (1945), 'Justice and the future of medicine', *Public Health Reports*, **60**, (5 January)

Bruce, I. (1993), *Pointers to the Future, Charity Talks on Successful Development*, Volprof, City University Business School

Caines, E. (1994), 'Plenty of scope for professional treatment', *The Times* (27 January)

Carrington, D. (1994), 'Understanding and managing risk,' paper from 1994 Charity Seminar, South Bank Business School and Charity Finance Directors' Group

Central Statistical Office (1993), *Charities' Contribution to Gross Domestic Product, Economic Trends No 482*, HMSO

Charity Commissioners (1994), *Annual Report of the Charity Commissioners 1993*, HMSO

CIMA (1992), *Return on Capital Employed Techniques in the NHS*, CIMA management accounting guides for the NHS

CIMA (1993), 'Performance management in executive agencies: an introduction', paper prepared for the Public Services Committee of the Chartered Institute of Management Accountants, April

Fitzgerald, L., Johnston, R., Brignall, S., Silvestro, R. and Voss, C. (1991), *Performance Measurement in Service Businesses*, CIMA

Friedman, M. (1980), *Free to Choose*, Penguin

Gutch, R. (1992), *Contracting Lessons from the US*, NCVO Publications

Harrison, J. (1994), *Managing Charitable Investments*, ICSA Publishing

Hill, R. *et al.* (1988), *A Wider Vision: The management and organisation of services for people who are blind or visually handicapped*, Social Services Inspectorate, Department of Health and Social Security

Hind, A. (1994), 'Understanding and managing risk', paper from 1994 Charity Seminar, South Bank Business School and Charity Finance Directors' Group.

HM Treasury (1991), *Competing for Quality: Buying better public services* (Cm. 1730), HMSO

HM Treasury (1994), *Better Accounting for the Taxpayer's Money: Resource accounting and budgeting in government* (Cm. 2626), HMSO

Home Office (1989), *Charities: A framework for the future* (Cm. 694), HMSO

Home Office Voluntary Services Unit (1995), *Accounting by Charities: Consultation on the draft regulations*, January

House of Commons Treasury and Civil Service Committee (1982), *Efficiency and Effectiveness in the Civil Service: Government observations on the third report*, 3 vols (Session 1981–82, HC 236, Cmnd. 8616), HMSO

Hyndman, N. and Anderson, R. (1991), 'Public sector accounting: looking beyond financial reporting', *Management Accounting*, 1991

Jenkins, S. (1994), 'Proposal that beggars belief', *The Times* (1 June)

Kaye, J. (1993), *Foundations of Corporate Success*, London Business School

Knight, B. (1993), *Voluntary Action*, Home Office, London

Leat, D. (1993), *Managing Across Sectors*, City University, London

Lloyd, T. (1993), *The Charity Business*, John Murray

Manley, K. (1994), *Financial Management for Charities and Voluntary Organisations*, ICSA Publishing

Matheson, J. (1990), 'Voluntary Work', General Household Survey 1987, Office of Population Censuses and Surveys, series GHS, no. 17, supplement A, HMSO

Meyer, C. (1994), 'How the right measures help teams excel', *Harvard Business Review, May–June*

Mullin, R. (1995), *Foundations for Fundraising*, ICSA Charities Management Series

NCVO (1981), 'Report of the Handy working party on improving effectiveness in voluntary organisations', interim conclusions, January

NCVO (1990), *Effectiveness and the Voluntary Sector*, Report of a Working Party, Chairman Lord Nathan

Open University (1993), *Performance Measurement and Evaluation*, Course B889

Parris, M. (1994), 'Monster that stalks Highgate', *The Times* (25 June)

Porter, M.E. (1979), 'How competitive forces shape strategy', *Harvard Business Review*, March/April

Presland, T. (n.d.), *Mission Statements: Values, practice and the contract culture, Part II*, The Volunteer Centre UK

Rankin, M. (n.d.), *Mission Statement, Values and Practice, Part I*, The Volunteer Centre UK

Smith, J.L. (1995), 'Has this man unlocked the secrets of happy marriage?', *The Times* (22 February)

Snoddy, R. (1994), 'Lottery rapped on fundraising efficiency', *Financial Times* (14 October)

Westwick, C.A. (1973), *How to Use Management Ratios – A Gower Workbook*, Gower Press

Wise, D.E. (1994), 'Charities management information survey', September/October, unpublished research paper

Index